FOOTBALL'S TWIN-I:
A COMPLETE
MULTIPLE OPTION
ATTACK

FOOTBALL'S TWIN-I: A COMPLETE MULTIPLE OPTION ATTACK

Doug Bluth

Parker Publishing Company, Inc.   West Nyack, New York

© 1984, *by*

PARKER PUBLISHING COMPANY, INC.
West Nyack, N.Y.

Library of Congress Cataloging in Publication Data

Bluth, Doug.
  Football's Twin-I.

  Includes index.
  1. Football—Offense. 2. Football—Coaching.
I. Title.
GV951.8.B63   1984   796.332'2   84-3138

ISBN 0-13-324302-8

Printed in the United States of America

DEDICATION

To my most loyal fan—my loving wife Susan—for all her encouragement, patience, and devotion.

To our children—Melanie, Jennie, and Mac—they are the pride and purpose of our lives.

To Mac and Thelma Bluth—exceptional parents whose values are rooted in honesty, sincerity, and commitment.

To Coach Max Spilsbury—a mountain of a man whose gentle persuasion and energetic example has given direction and purpose to the lives of so many young men.

ACKNOWLEDGMENTS

I wish to express my sincere appreciation to the many good friends, athletes, and associates who have contributed more than they can know toward the development and the success of the Twin-I Multiple Option concept that resulted in this manuscript. Any system is only as successful as the degree of commitment made by those who put on the uniform and strive for excellence. Athletes such as Barry Laga, Craig Swapp, Steve Warner, Brian Tobler, Craig Hilton, Clark Hill, Curt Harrison, Leo Biggs—and all the young men who were completely selfless, totally devoted, and deeply committed to winning—give coaching a special meaning.

Good assistant coaches are priceless. A special thanks is credited to Darold Henry and Scott Ormond. Their genuine personalities have contributed in so many ways to the success of this program.

A solid administration is essential for all developing programs. I am especially grateful for the direction and support rendered by Principal Tom Carlile. His seemingly endless positive views and comments have been highly motivational for the staff, players, and community.

And finally, an exclusive and personal tribute to Julie Hansen, who volunteered countless hours to type the original drafts of this manuscript.

HOW THE TWIN-I
MULTIPLE OPTION
WILL HELP YOU WIN

The offensive trend in football today is without a doubt the option attack. However, this trend is challenged by the need to become wide open and diversified to remain competitive. The triple option is as exciting today as it always has been, but its effectiveness as a single series attack has been greatly nullified by the advancements in defensive game planning. The Twin-I Multiple Option counters defensive genius with an exciting balance between a multiple selection of basic option series and a finely tuned option passing game.

The Twin-I Multiple Option will introduce you to the advantages of the I backfield as possibly the best backfield from which to execute most option series. There are currently many option attacks all marketed from a variety of backfields (i.e., splitback, wishbone, power I, and several tandem sets). The Twin-I backfield is not new, but it is revolutionary in option football. Its flexibility is unparalleled. This formation gives the offense many advantages not offered from other alignments. This book gives a precise introduction to the Option I backfield, together with a comparison to its leading rivals.

The Twin-I Multiple Option also incorporates the best overall passing alignment, that of twin receivers. Twin receivers create not only explosive running potential, but an overwhelming pass threat to the defense. Both the experienced and novice coach will be able to use this book as a technical manual for keeping the defense off balance with a devastating running attack that not only is complemented by, but continually capitalizes on, an explosive passing arsenal. Together, the option and the wide open pass produce the highest scoring offenses in modern football. The Twin-I Multiple Option is a premier blend of wide open, exciting, high-scoring football.

Most written material on option football currently on the market is geared primarily for the situations where the key to success is recruiting to fill each position with a particular type of athlete. For some time, option football in its truest form has been thought of as too difficult for high-school players and has remained primarily at advanced levels. The Twin-I Multiple Option is formulated to give the high-school coach a creative option offense which is as flexible as the talent available from year to year. This book will share detailed fundamentals and techniques which can be applied directly to the high-school skill level. Along with these explicit techniques, supporting concepts and objectives are matched to give you a balanced approach to install this multiple option offense.

This text is written for the high-school coach who is interested in adopting a multiple option as a complete offense or in simply selecting from this package a single series or option concept to incorporate into an already established program. This book offers any interested coach the opportunity for professional enhancement through familiarization of current option trends and the challenge to experiment with a fascinating offense whose limits are virtually unexplored.

Option football is getting bigger and better, and this text will take you through a step-by-step approach of how to select the right personnel for each position. A special emphasis is dedicated to the selection and training of the young option quarterback. The current drills and techniques that make the Twin-I Multiple Option highly successful are explained. Questions are raised throughout the text about the fundamental concepts of option football. Each is answered in clear, precise, technical terms. However, this book is unique in that it takes you beyond the standardized answers. This text presents the next most important step, that of the administration of proper drills, which teach the fundamental techniques that make option football sensational.

Defenses have always dreaded preparing for the option. The basic nature of the option takes away radical defensive pursuit, the backbone of all defenses. The Twin-I Multiple Option will overpower defenses with the triple option. Complementary option series such as the counter trap option and the crazy option will keep the same defenses neutralized. A full scope of successful play-action pass series are presented to cement the effectiveness of this strategic offense. An option attack, coupled with a dynamically simple option-passing game, makes this offense a pleasure to coach, exciting to play, and thrilling to watch.

The best defense in football is a great offensive attack. Your opponent cannot beat you if he does not possess the football. The Twin-I Multiple Option is premier tempo control football. You will learn to attack the defense vertically and horizontally, and to force your opponent to defend every square foot of grass every snap of the ball. You will outcoach your opponent by installing the ultimate offensive weapon, a complete multiple option attack. The trend in winning football is the high-scoring offense. You can meet this challenge with the explosive Twin-I Multiple Option offense.

Doug Bluth

TABLE OF CONTENTS

EXPLODING
WITH THE TWIN-I
FORMATION

The triple option can be credited for having provided some of the most explosive offensive football in modern gridiron history. No other single offense has produced the controversy and excitement as has option football. Many styles of offense rise to prominence and then disappear, leaving little in their wake except nostalgic recollections.

The true test of the great offense is its adaptability to new defensive strategies. Football as a sport has emerged through a renaissance of changing philosophies. What was once a simple sport is now a complex science. The use of computers and other mechanical aids have increased the performance levels of coaching staffs. Science has graced athletics with new horizons in sports medicine and performance training that produce a more effective athlete. These advances applied to the evolution of defensive football have challenged the effectiveness of every offense. Some offenses have survived, others have become obsolete.

The genealogy of option football can be traced through each defensive advancement. Option concepts can be found in almost every offensive system. The basic objective of the option attack is to take advantage of defensive commitment after the snap of the ball. Many offenses adopt option concepts to create intrinsic flexibility to counter defensive strategies. One example is the sprint draw

series from the I formation. The concept of giving the ball carrier a
point of attack (POA) choice based upon defensive pursuit is fundamental option theory. Another example is observed in passing
team philosophies. The popular "option screen" has become an
effective weapon for optioning defenses on a vertical scale. Reading coverages by quarterbacks (QBs) and receivers is nothing more
than a method of taking advantage of defensive post-snap commitment.

WHY INCORPORATE AN OPTION ATTACK?

There are several reasons that can be listed for supporting the
position that the multiple option is one answer to unique offensive
problems faced in many football programs. Adaptability to available personnel must be the foremost reason considered.

Personnel of average size and skill can be taught to successfully execute an option offense. The "big" lineman who possesses
raw power and strength is not a prerequisite for effective blocking
schemes. Option football is a finesse rather than a power offense.
Therefore, there is little need to drive back defenders or root them
out of a designated POA. The objective of option blocking, discussed in Chapter 6, is to neutralize defenders in and along the line
of scrimmage (LOS).

Many coaches incorrectly assume that the option requires the
above average athlete to perform as the QB. There are certain
characteristics (i.e., leadership, competitiveness, coachability, etc.)
that must be evident, but most option techniques that are required
can be taught with success to the athlete who would normally
qualify as QB material. However, even though a successful option
attack can be built with less than superior personnel, it is an un-
avoidable fact that the more superior the personnel available, the
more potential this offensive package will have.

An option attack takes away from the defense that one ingre-
dient that makes all defenses effective—pursuit. The option is
capable of attacking the LOS on a complete horizontal scale. The
threat of the dive, the QB keep, or the wide pitch forces defenses to
play assignment football, as opposed to the basic toss sweep play,
where the ball is committed immediately very deep in the backfield.
The defense can now react to rehearsed keys pursuing quickly
toward the LOS.

Against the triple option, the defense must now respect each
of the potential ball carriers at his assigned POA along the LOS.

Any over- or under-defensive pursuit creates an offensive edge. The triple option is not dependent upon raw power to move the football. Slowing down defensive pursuit is done with deception. Unlike the toss sweep, where the ball is declared deep in the backfield, the triple option operates up near the LOS, generating momentum that quickly capitalizes on defensive error.

The triple option is a quick-hitting offense that directly attacks the LOS. Ball handling is kept to minimum. The basic blocking schemes are simple and have a high degree of consistency in application to a wide variety of defensive fronts. More practice time can be devoted to perfecting fundamental techniques once the basic triple option series is learned; the carryover concepts are applied to the complementary option series. Such series as counter option, trap, and lead option are easily adopted since the basic concepts and techniques are utilized.

The option running game is so dynamic that defenses often become vulnerable to the play-action pass. Defenders are required to outnumber the option in the direction of offensive flow. This forces a solid commitment by the secondary to come up and take on a block near the LOS. When the defensive secondary commits toward the LOS, it becomes vulnerable to the forward pass. Passing the football is often thought of as an unnecessary skill in dominant option circles. This is not the case. Option football depends upon its ability to keep defenses off balance. The secondary must be kept conscious of the fact that the ball may be thrown on any down.

ADVANTAGES OF THE I BACKFIELD

Selecting a backfield alignment from which to execute the triple option is an issue which should be studied. Too often, the entire option package that is selected is done so because of current popularity. Popularity is not always related to success; therefore, emulation is the downfall of many programs. The triple option executed from the I backfield has many unique advantages not found in other alignments.

Simplicity in teaching an offense should be a foremost consideration. Short cuts to learning should be sought for and designed into the offensive package. Learning the option from the I backfield is unilateral. This means the fullback (FB) will be the diveback to either side, and the tailback (TB) functions as the pitchback to both sides of the formation. This cuts directional learning in half and does not give a directional tendency to the defense. The QB becomes accustomed to the speed of the FB's mesh action. This reduces hesitation in the ride/decide phase in technique performance. The TB's speed to the corner is consistent for the pitch angle. These timing factors play an important role in practicing and perfecting a successful option attack.

Each person in the I backfield can be selected to fit positional requirements. Since the FB will always be the diveback, he can be selected for his inside running and ball control abilities. Likewise, the TB will need to exhibit skills in handling the pitch and in open field running. There are no directional tendencies surrendered to the defense when these two positions are constantly aligned in the I formation. This differs from the split backfield, where if only one quality diveback is available, a directional tendency is given if the diveback is changed from side to side of the formation.

Two other advantages of an I option backfield are as follows. First, there can now be three receivers placed upon or near the LOS in quick-release positions. The fact that only three positions are required in the backfield allows great freedom for overall formation experimentation. Second, the presence of three quick receivers eliminates defensive nine-man fronts. Many option defenses commit nine people to the LOS to contain the running game and assign two defenders to man coverage on outside receivers. The threat of three quick receivers reduces the nine-man front to an eight- or seven-man front. The running game now has a chance to succeed.

Another key advantage is the two-point stance taken by the TB. Many wishbone teams are requiring their halfbacks to assume a two-point stance. This stance permits the pitchbacks to better read defensive keys. The TB in the I backfield uses a two-point stance for precisely this reason. Reading defensive pre-snap alignment and post-snap reaction is imperative if the perimeter running lanes are to be challenged quickly.

The I is a balanced backfield. There is no declaration of strength or directional tendency offered. The Power I, for example, declares a strength alignment with the position of the upback. Executing the triple option into the formation strength is technically sound. However, optioning into the weak side requires certain formation or technique adjustments. If the TB is to remain as the pitchback, the upback must either shift opposite prior to the snap or motion across the formation. Should the option be run into the weak side with no adjustment, the upback's blocking advantage has been lost.

The popularity of the I backfield has spread nationally, probably because of its adaptability to such a wide variety of offensive series. Sweeps, powers, isolations, traps, and TB counters are only a few of the I backfield's capabilities. Each have their own merits, but the triple option and its complementary series from the I alignment possess marked advantages over other backfields, primarily through inherent geometry.

The geometry of the I backfield creates several unique advantages that aid in teaching the triple option. The first technical fundamental which will be discussed is the QB/FB mesh, along with its relation to the ride/decide phase of the triple option. Diagrams 1-1 through 1-4 compare specific advantages of the I FB ride/decide technique to those of the split backfield.

The proximity of the QB to the collision point on the LOS during the ride/decide phase of the option is a critical issue. The I QB is much further removed from the dive read point (Diagram 1-1) than is the splitback QB (Diagram 1-2). The young QB is granted more time to make an accurate give/disconnect read with the diving FB. This longer ride time creates more deception, thus holding inside defenders closer to the LOS. Slowing down defensive pursuit prevents the inside LBers from outnumbering the option at the perimeter. The longer ride also gives the FB an accurate pressure read to interpret the QB's give or disconnect signal. Establishing confidence in the QB/FB mesh and ride is the number one priority in installing the Twin-I option.

Next, the FB's dive lane must be considered. The I FB is able to attack the LOS at a consistent angle. Any cutback or change of running lane directions will occur down beyond the LOS. The splitback FB is required to change directions in the LOS. In many

   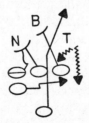

Diagram 1-1   **Diagram 1-2**

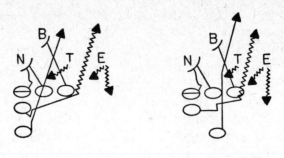

Diagram 1-3   **Diagram 1-4**

instances, this change of direction coincides with the ball exchanges. The I FB is able to control the ball long before a change of direction is necessary.

Attacking the option point (OP) after the disconnect from the FB is a critical phase in triple option format. Disconnecting from the I FB places the QB further away from the keep/pitch read. This distance gives the young QB time to regain balance and make the final option read correctly. Diagrams 1-3 and 1-4 illustrate the proximity of the two QBs to the option point. The splitback QB must execute all three option reads in a fraction of a second. The I QB not only has more time to execute the triple reads, but also has a more functional angle in attacking downhill toward the option point.

The triple option's main objective is to get the pitch on the corner. All blocking schemes are designed to break the big play up the sideline. Aligning the pitchback (PB) at a depth of seven yards in the I formation gives the triple option a strategic edge. At a depth of seven yards and in a balanced alignment, the PB is able to get to the corner quicker. This virtually eliminates the *feathering,* or slow-playing defensive end technique. This defender cannot play both the QB and the PB if the TB has turned the pitch route and is attacking the LOS at the moment of the pitch.

Diagrams 1-5 and 1-6 demonstrate the relationship between the QB and the PB after disconnecting from the FB. Both QBs face a crashing defensive end. The I PB is in an arc outside the DE with his hips turning toward the LOS. The splitback PB is still running parallel to the LOS at the moment of the pitch. He must still get to the perimeter and turn his hips upfield before he is considered an offensive weapon. To place the splitback PB in the outside pitch angle, tremendous speed is required. This caliber of speed is not

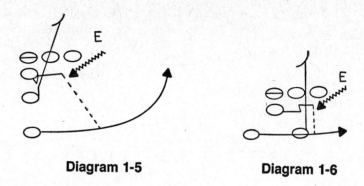

Diagram 1-5   Diagram 1-6

consistently present in most programs. A skilled running back with good speed can be very effective at the PB position from the I alignment.

ADVANTAGES OF THE TWIN RECEIVER ALIGNMENT

Any formation that is used to create an offensive package must be selected for its technical value rather than for its popularity status. The flexibility of the formation must be considered. Can the formation be adjusted to capitalize on each offensive situation that is encountered during the vertical progression of the ball? Can the formation dictate defensive alignment? Does the formation create an offensive blocking design advantage? Does the formation provide a balanced opportunity to execute both the running and passing games? The twin formation positively satisfies the above criteria.

The twin alignment by design prevents the defense from aligning in a nine-man front. The possibility of three quick receivers getting deep immediately dictates that if the defense is to be sound, at least three defenders must be aligned in the secondary prior to the snap.

Wishbone teams constantly face nine-man fronts (Diagram 1-7) because there are only two quick receivers. The twin alignment not only prevents the nine-man front, but also encourages the reduction of an eight-man front to a seven-man front. The twin alignment creates a severe crack block angle on the 44 defense's stacked outside LB (Diagram 1-8). The twin alignment invites the eight-man front LB to walk away into a more direct pitch support alignment. The twin receiver combination also encourages a pre-invert strong safety from four deep defenses. Diagram 1-9 illustrates a 52 defense aligned in a pre-invert. Both the walkaway LB and the pre-inverted safety declare defensive option assignment before the snap.

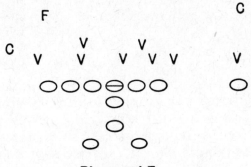

Diagram 1-7

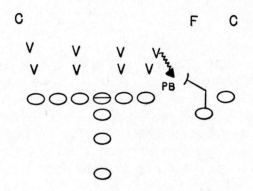

Diagram 1-8

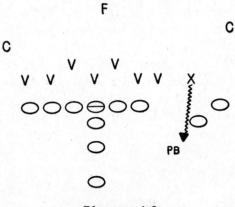

Diagram 1-9

The twin receiver formation spreads the defense over a broad base front. This spread formation forces the defense to cover the entire field so that the secondary is stretched to capacity. The primary concept of the Twin-I is to force the defense to commit (by alignment) its option assignments either before the snap or immediately after.

Blocking angles created by the twin alignment are highly advantageous. Anytime perimeter receivers can be given direct block angles down to the inside, the perimeter running game has a good chance for success. Diagrams 1-10 and 1-11 demonstrate the value of a crack angle in the execution of the lead option. In both situations the widest defender must be driven off to prevent a corner roll. The slot receiver in Diagram 1-10 is able to position

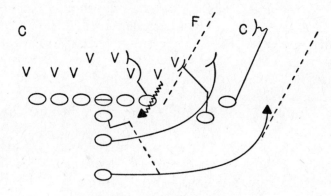

Diagram 1-10   Vs. Split 60

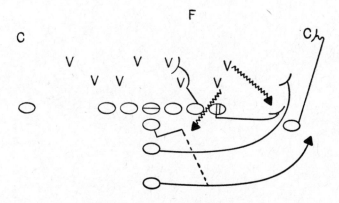

Diagram 1-11   Vs. Split 60

down on the pitch-support defender. This crack block prevents the defender from playing the pitch from the inside-out. The sideline crease can be effectively sealed. The TE in Diagram 1-11 must meet the same defender on the LOS, then battle for blocking position. This is a more difficult block to execute. Creating position blocking schemes for base and alternate series will increase the productivity of the option attack.

Having two quick receivers isolated to one side of the offensive formation creates a pass pattern arsenal. The two receivers can be used in a multitude of combination routes. Not only do they exhibit a quick pass pattern combination, but the twin receivers represent strongside blocking capabilities. Defenses cannot leave the alignment uncovered. In order to defense an eight-man front, either the secondary must balance up (Diagram 1-12), or a walkaway LB must be assigned pitch and flat coverage (Diagram 1-13).

The TE complements the formation in three ways. First, the TE can be aligned in a variety of distances from the OT to give the formation a creative edge in dictating defensive alignment. A twelve-yard split spreads a defense across the entire field. The three-yard flex creates problems for aligning defensive ends or outside stacks. The ability to radically change the formation by moving only one position is added evidence for the flexibility of the Twin-I.

Second, the TE's normal alignment creates strongside blocking capabilities. The TE is able to release inside on double-team blocks, or outside on stalk blocks. From a spread alignment the TE is able to stalk block deep or crack to the inside. Defenses must respect the blocking capabilities into the weak side of the formation.

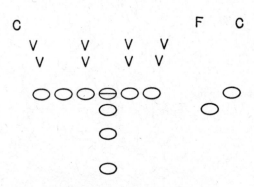

Diagram 1-12   Vs. 44 Stack

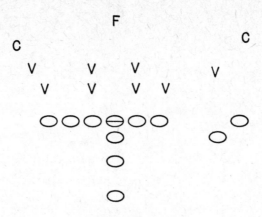

Diagram 1-13

Third, the TE cannot be ignored as a potential pass threat. Defenses cannot overrotate into the Twin side without leaving throwback seams for the TE. The flexibility of the TE's alignment complements all phases of the passing game.

The twin receiver alignment creates an opportunity for a motion package that is simple to teach and strategically effective. However, motion must be used for practical reasons. Motion must serve a specific purpose. Motion, in the Twin-I system, cannot be justified for cosmetic reasons. The Twin-I incorporates motion for the following reasons:

1. To change the strength of the formation;
2. To force a change in coverage;
3. To create a personnel advantage (i.e., a quicker slot receiver over a slower, less skilled defensive corner);
4. To cause confusion in defensive option support assignments;
5. To stretch the secondary from sideline to sideline;
6. And finally, as a decoy.

Three basic patterns of motion are essential to gain a strategic edge. Diagram 1-14 illustrates a full motion termed "Fly." The slot receiver's motion changes the strength of the formation. Diagram 1-14 also illustrates a complementing half motion termed "Zip." Zip places the inside receiver into a tight slot alignment for blocking or route release purposes. The slot is also aligned to release into the backfield into a pitchback assignment. The third motion scheme is

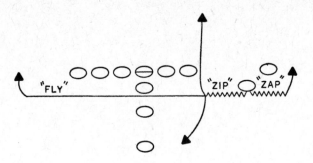

Diagram 1-14

termed "Zap." Zap motion puts the slot receiver outside of the split end. This scheme forces coverage change and complete secondary realignment.

The twin receiver alignment offers great strategic versatility. Blocking angles and pass pattern possibilities are of foremost importance in establishing a balanced offensive attack. The uniqueness of a simple motion package adds tremendous variety to the offense and increases defensive anxieties.

IDENTIFYING DEFENSIVE FRONTS

The twin receiver formation invites defensive front variations that have been designed to defend the option. Therefore, it is clearly important that defensive fronts be recognized and categorized. The primary need for recognition aids in identifying the defenders that will be optioned.

Categorizing defensive fronts determines how and where option support will come from. The eight-man front, such as the 53 in Diagram 1-15, aligns eight primary defenders near the LOS. This eight-man front forces the dive and QB from the outside-in, but attacks the pitch from the inside-out. The 44 stack in Diagram 1-16 illustrates only the QB being forced from the outside-in. Eight-man fronts, as a general rule, are strong against the inside phase of the option. However, the QB keep and pitch phase stands a good chance of succeeding.

The seven-man front (Diagram 1-17) such as the 52 aligns seven defenders near the LOS. The strength of the seven-man front is that all phases of the option can be forced from the outside-

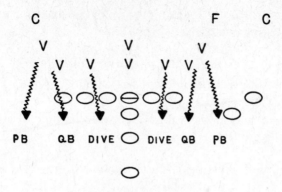

Diagram 1-15

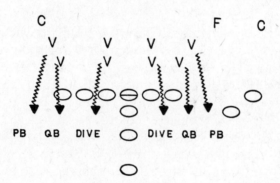

Diagram 1-16

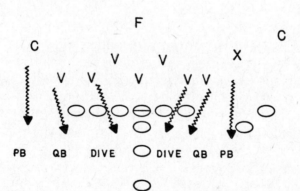

Diagram 1-17

in. Categorizing the defensive alignment as either a seven- or an eight-man front serves three functions:

1. It helps predict defensive option assignments prior to the snap.
2. It helps determine which phase or phases of the option will be defended heaviest.
3. It helps determine weaknesses in the secondary to facilitate the passing game.

Next, the defense must be categorized as either an even or an odd man front. This analysis is critical for two reasons:

1. It helps identify the dive read and the keep/pitch read.
2. It helps to determine the most productive option blocking schemes.

An even front is recognized when the center is uncovered. The center is now able to assist to either gap or to attack downfield to cut off LB pursuit. The most critical gap that must be blocked is the center-guard gap. The center's block must insure the QB's clearance into the OG-OT gap. Identifying the even man front expands the center's range of mobility.

The odd front places a defender directly over the center on the LOS. Blocking schemes must now be designed to prevent the noseguard from slanting through the center-guard gap. The odd front places strain on initial ball exchange and the QB/FB ride. Option blocking schemes must be designed from the inside-out. After the center's block is assured, corresponding option blocking assignments can be designed.

NUMBERING DEFENSIVE FRONTS

Numbering the defensive front serves two major purposes:

1. Numbering simplifies blocking assignments.
2. Numbering quickly isolates the defenders that will be optioned.

Each defense will be numbered two ways: first, from the inside-out, and second, from the outside-in.

A numerical assignment is given to the interior defenders. This simplifies line blocking assignments. The defender over the center, or the defender blocked by the center is assigned zero (Diagram 1-18). Each succeeding defender is then numbered from the inside-out. In the case of a stack (Diagram 1-19), the defender on the LOS is given the lower number.

The interior numbering is critical in identifying the defenders that will be optioned. As a general rule, versus a seven-man front number two is the dive read and three is the keep/pitch read. Versus an eight-man front, numbers three and four assume corresponding values.

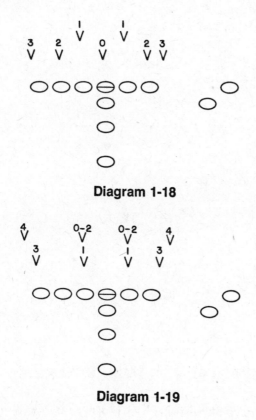

Diagram 1-18

Diagram 1-19

The perimeter is numbered from the outside-in strictly for receiver blocking assignment recognition. To eliminate confusion, these defenders are assigned ordinal numbers. The widest defenders are designated as the first. Then each position is added on thereafter (Diagram 1-20). Versus a three-deep secondary (Diagram 1-21), the safety is counted as the second defender to both sides. The third defender is generally the QB's keep/pitch read.

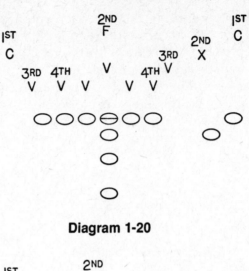

Diagram 1-20

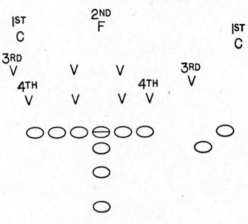

Diagram 1-21

DETERMINING WHERE TO RUN

There are two criteria that dictate where the ball should be run. The first one is taking advantage of weak defensive personnel, and the second one is locating alignment weaknesses left by defensive balance. The former needs no elaboration; therefore the latter is examined.

When the Twin-I formation is cut in half, the formation aligns with eight positions to the strong side and seven to the weak (Diagram 1-22). Using this counting method as a tool, defenses can be counted to verify a balanced alignment. Diagram 1-23 illustrates

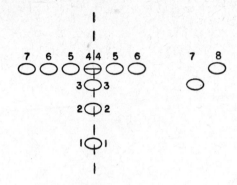

Diagram 1-22

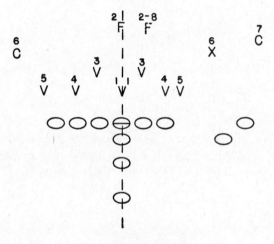

Diagram 1-23

a 52 defense which is balanced in design. Any balanced defense will number seven to the formation's strength and six into the weak side. The offensive formation has gained a one-man advantage to either side. This defensive front can balance up to the formation by sliding the free safety over to either side. This, however, creates a two-man advantage to the vacated side for the offense.

The triple option is capable of accounting for the first four ordinal defenders in the perimeter. The first and second are blocked, the third and fourth are optioned. If the defense commits a fifth, the option is outnumbered. Diagram 1-24 shows a weakside overshift that has the option outnumbered. The FS has an uncontested pitch-support assignment. This same defensive alignment, however, has given up a three-man advantage into the strong side

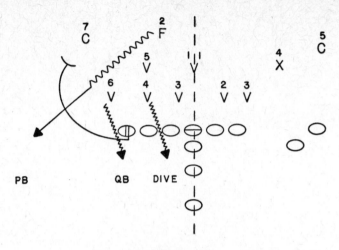

Diagram 1-24

of the formation. The option now stands a good chance of succeeding away from the defensive shift.

In summary, the option running attack must be directed toward that part of the defense which has a numbering disadvantage. A balanced defense gives the offense great latitude toward either side. The unbalanced defense is a gambling alignment. The option must be directed away from the fifth defender.

DETERMINING WHERE TO PASS

There are three phases of the Twin-I passing package: play-action, quick pass, and the open passing attack. Where to throw the ball is as important to know as how to throw. The Twin-I incorporates three primary criteria in selecting where to throw the football. First, weak personnel in the secondary are isolated and challenged. Second, weaknesses left in secondary alignment are found, and third, vacated zones left when secondary personnel commit to support the option are located. The second and third criteria are the most critical to develop since personnel advantage is not a norm.

Weakness in defensive alignment can easily be recognized versus the Twin-I formation. Diagram 1-25 illustrates a three-deep secondary that has not balanced up to the twin receivers. This creates a two-on-one offensive edge. The "soft spot" in the coverage is quickly identified. The same three-deep (Diagram 1-26) has

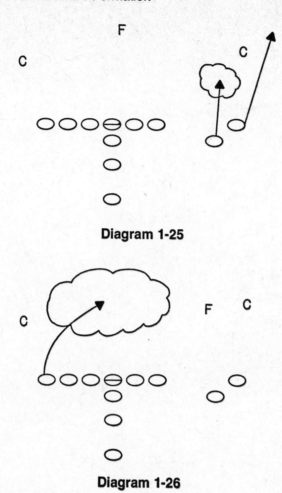

Diagram 1-25

Diagram 1-26

balanced up to the twin receivers. A large spot has now been created deep over the middle. Defensive horizontal balance can be monitored quickly by identifying the coverage to the twin side. The quick pass (Diagram 1-27) capitalizes on defensive vertical misalignment. A secondary unit, or an individual defender that aligns ten yards or deeper, opens up the short quick pass seams.

The triple option commands run support from the defense. Option support from the secondary vacates throwing seams. Diagram 1-28 illustrates a strong safety supporting the pitch. A soft spot is created by his forward support. Corner roll support (Diagrams 1-29 and 1-30), leaves soft spots in the perimeter of the secondary. This three quick receiver concept not only creates perimeter blocking advantages, but *dictates* to the defensive secondary that pass coverage is their first responsibility.

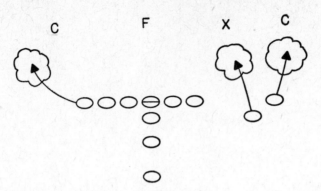

Diagram 1-27

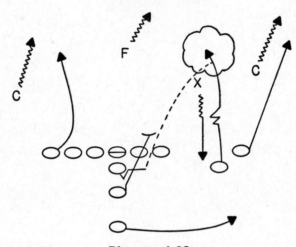

Diagram 1-28

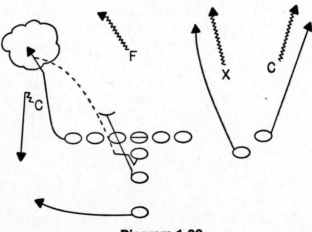

Diagram 1-29

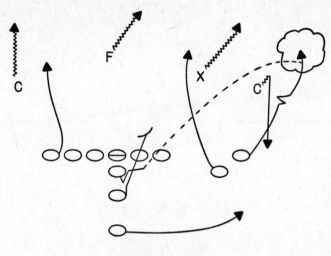

Diagram 1-30

2

INSTALLING
THE TWIN-I SYSTEM

There are five fundamental aspects of the Twin-I system that collectively construct a flexible yet simple package. Naming positions, numbering the points of attack, formationing splits and concepts, and numbering the series are each kept in a simple format that makes learning the complete system practical and functional.

NAMING THE TWIN-I POSITIONS

The Twin-I system keeps each position's name relative to its assignment and function. The interior personnel are the center, the guards, and the tackles (to the center's right and left). No distinction is made as to "weak" or "strong" side personnel. Rule blocking and the point of attack determine which is the "onside" and "offside" of the formation. This system requires the interior five to become familiar with both the onside and offside blocking techniques and assignment. Defenses are unable to detect directional tendencies that may be presented in flip-flop or strongside-weakside systems.

Diagram 2-1 illustrates the basic Twin-I right formation. The SE, or Z, aligns to the strong side of the formation on the LOS. The slot (SLT), or Y, aligns one yard off the LOS inside of the SE. These

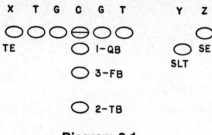

Diagram 2-1

two receivers are the foundation of the Twin alignment. The TE, or *X*, aligns opposite of *Y* and *Z* to complete the weak side of the formation. The I backfield alignment consists of the QB, who is designated as 1, the FB as 3, and the TB as 2. Each perimeter and backfield position is assigned two names. The first is an alignment or position name, and the second is a play selection title.

The play selection title is assigned to receiver and backfield positions to simplify play calling in the huddle. Referring to the TE as *X* saves considerable time in calling a selective pass route that incorporates the TE. Each position can be included in combination pass patterns with considerable ease. Blocking or option assignments become less complicated when each position can be quickly identified.

NUMBERING THE POINTS OF ATTACK

The Twin-I system assigns even numbers to the formation's right side, and odd numbers to the left (Diagram 2-2). Each point of attack (POA) is assigned directly over an offensive position. The numbering begins from the inside-out by splitting the center in half. The center's right leg is "zero" and his left is "one." Numbering each position (rather than the gap) with a definite right-left

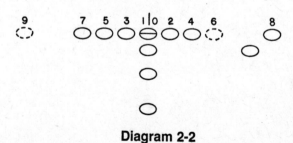

Diagram 2-2

distinction creates a clear picture for both play direction and the
POA. This distinction reduces backfield errors in landmark selection. The FB can easily identify the OG's alignment prior to the
snap should the series call for diving action. Even though the OG
will move on the snap, his original position serves as the POA
landmark.

The point of attack must be clearly defined in each offensive
series. Numbering each position creates a vivid picture for interior
blocking patterns. Identifying a specific landmark as the POA also
polishes the techniques and mechanics of each series. Directing the
attack at either the six or seven hole is much more specific than
directing the attack "off tackle."

SPLITS AND SPACING FOR THE TWIN-I FORMATION

The general formation splits and position spacing are illustrated in Diagram 2-3. The OGs assume a two-and-one-half-foot
split from the center. The tackles continue out to a full three-foot
split from the guards. Along with these spacing guidelines, the
interior four positions must crowd the LOS. It is imperative that
both guards and tackles align on the LOS. Each lineman's down
hand must be as close to the back end of the football as possible.
There are three reasons for aligning the Twin-I lineman upon the
LOS. First, the lineman can explode into and beyond the neutral
zone much faster. Second, this quick surge is able to block defensive
stunts before they develop. Third, the movement into the neutral
zone creates a downhill angle along the LOS for the QB to execute
the optioning techniques.

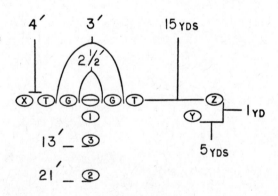

Diagram 2-3

The receiver's splits and spacing are more flexible than those of the interior line. The TE aligns four feet outside of the tackle. The SE aligns no more than fifteen yards from the tackle but never closer than six yards to the sideline. This six-yard cushion from the sideline gives the SE room for outbreaking routes. The SLT takes his alignment from the SE. The SLT splits five yards inside of the SE and one yard off the LOS. It is critical that both Y and Z keep this spacing constant. The timing for blocking angles and pass patterns is dependent upon a consistent alignment.

The base I backfield spacing aligns the TB's feet at a seven-yard depth. This specific depth is critical in predicting the TB's proper pitch route release. This seven-yard depth also gives the TB good counter dive momentum. The TB can gain a perimeter blocking angle for the full-sprint pass series (Diagram 2-4).

The FB aligns his heels, as a general rule, at thirteen feet. This is an arbitrary depth that is dependent upon the FB's starting speed. Should the FB be slower in starting, a half step forward polishes the QB mesh and ride.

There are three factors that affect the general splits and spacing of the basic formation. First is vertical field position. The second is horizontal field position, and the third is the defensive interior alignment. As the ball advances down the field, each of these criteria must be recognized as instrumental in spacing and alignment.

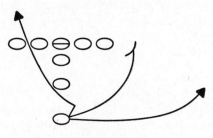

Diagram 2-4

The splits and spacing of the base formation relative to vertical field position is dependent upon defensive tendencies in each critical field zone. Tighter splits for the interior line may be necessary when coming out of the three-down conservative zone (Diagram 2-5). Controlling defensive stunts and games is critical when coming out from deep in negative yard position. A general tightening of the formation not only protects the development of the

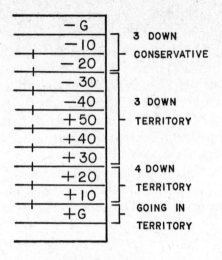

Diagram 2-5

option, but also tightens down pass routes for a more conservative passing game.

Both the three- and four-down territories represent the position for greatest formation flexibility. The offensive splits and spacing can now be relative to the offensive game plan. A less conservative profile is possible since a wider variety of offensive series may be incorporated.

The *going-in* territory requires a tightening of the interior splits for security reasons. Goal line defenses generally align in a gap control front. Wide interior splits invite defensive penetration. A tightening of the interior line represents security, not conservatism.

The horizontal field position primarily affects the receivers and their alignment. With the ball in the middle of the field (Diagram 2-6), the SE is able to take a full fifteen-yard split. The final decision for spacing is dependent upon blocking angles or pass route assignments.

When the ball is located on the hash mark with the Twin set into the wide side of the field (Diagram 2-7), the SE has the capability of taking a maximum split. This wide side alignment forces the defensive secondary to cover the complete field. Pass patterns and blocking assignments for the Twin receivers are complemented by this wide side spacing.

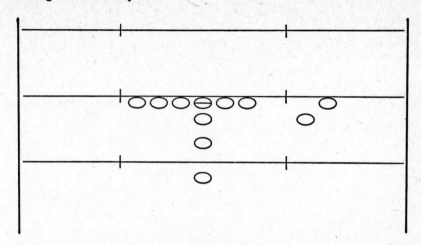

Diagram 2-6

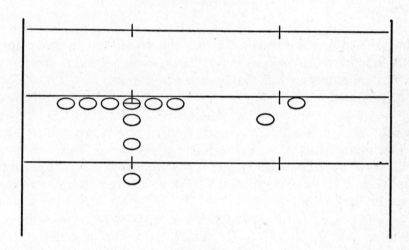

Diagram 2-7

Diagram 2-8 illustrates the formation aligned on the hash with the Twin receivers into the sideline. This situation radically condenses the formation. There are two primary adjustments needed in this situation. First, the SE must not align closer than six yards from the sideline. Second, the SLT must split the distance between the SE and the OT.

Defensive interior alignment becomes a critical issue in regard to option execution. The defensive interior alignment will dictate

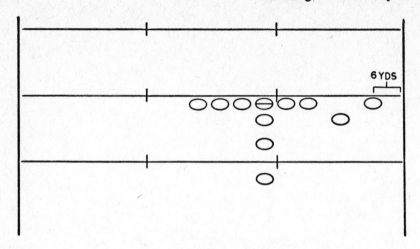

Diagram 2-8

which blocking schemes are used. There are two primary areas along the LOS that directly affect splits between the offensive line. The first area is the center-guard gap and the second is the alignment of the defender in the dive-read position.

As mentioned in Chapter 1, the center-guard gap is the focal point for assigning blocking schemes. This area must be secure against stunts, slants, or direct penetrating alignments. The center-guard splits must be reduced when facing an inside gap such as the 6-2 defense in Diagram 2-9. Reducing this split permits the OG to collision the gapped defender and prevents penetration into the backfield.

The position of the fourth defender (the dive-read) will dictate variation in the offensive tackle's split. The objective of the OT's split is to remove the fourth defender as far from the FB dive crease as possible. Diagram 2-10 depicts a 5–1 defense with the fourth defender aligned in an outside shoulder position. A four-foot split by the OT creates three offensive advantages:

1. A wider dive-read gives the QB maximum reading time during the FB ride.
2. The wide fourth defender must commit immediately upon the snap to his option assignment.
3. The OT has a direct inside release to seal pursuing LBers.

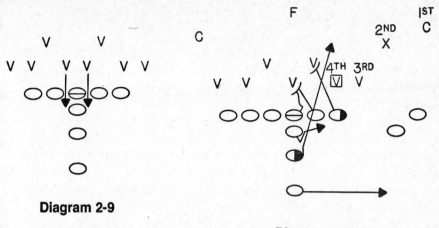

Diagram 2-9

Diagram 2-10

The OT must be prepared to reduce his split with the OG slightly when this gap is threatened by defensive alignment. Diagram 2-11 illustrates the fourth defender reduced down into the G-T gap. The OT now collisions this penetrating defender. In situations where the OT is assigned to *rub-double down* with the OG (Diagram 2-12), such as versus the split 60 defense, a slightly reduced split facilitates the blocking scheme. A flexible spacing between the interior linemen is imperative to protect the development of the option along the LOS.

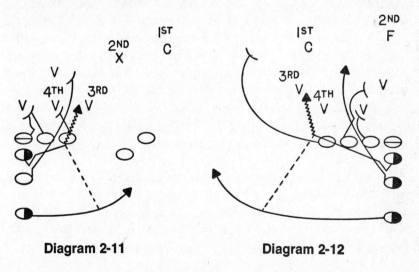

Diagram 2-11   **Diagram 2-12**

THE TWIN-I FORMATIONING CONCEPT

The concept of formationing can be defined as "the ability for an offensive formation to make minor alignment adjustments that create defensive weaknesses or neutralize defensive alignment strategies without radically altering the formation or related series assignments." Many offensive systems incorporate multiple formation alignments to gain an offensive advantage. The use of multiple formations is effective, but learning has also been multiplied. The Twin-I formationing concept is centered on creating an offensive pre-snap edge through minor formation adjustments, rather than utilizing completely different formations. There are three areas where formationing occurs. The first is through the adjustments into the formations and weak side. The second is the strongside SLT adjustments.

There are two primary TE formationing alignments. The flex formation (Diagram 2-13) aligns X at four yards. Moving the TE out to twelve yards (Diagram 2-14) creates the spread formation. There are three reasons for incorporating the flex formation. First, a four-yard split facilitates the TE release from the LOS. Diagram 2-15 illustrates the TE's ability to release inside on blocking schemes and on pass routes. Isolating the TE at four yards prevents his being jammed by covering defenders. The TE now has considerable freedom to release inside or outside.

Another advantage of the flex alignment is illustrated in Diagram 2-16. The four-yard split moves the DE farther outside. Widening the option point (OP) gives the QB more reading time after the disconnect from the FB. The third defender must immediately react to his option assignment on the snap. This quick commitment by the defender facilitates better option reads.

The third purpose for the flex has strategic implications. Diagram 2-17 illustrates a weakside 44 stack defense. The stack over the TE presents a difficult option read for the QB, especially if the stack stunts or exchanges option assignments at random. Flexing the TE now puts the pressure on the defense. The defense can keep the stack over the TE as diagramed in 2-18. Any stunting from this wide stack is ineffective. The QB has ample time to interpret the gaming action. Or, the defense may elect to align the stack inside the flex. Doing so creates a very quick crack block angle

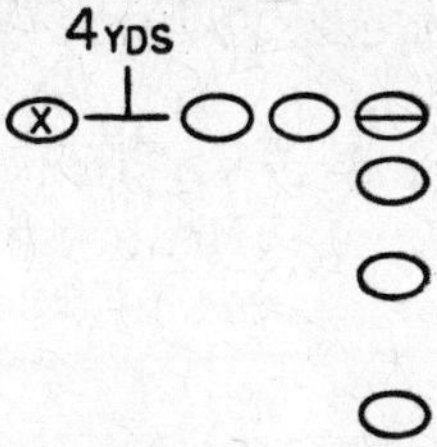

4 YDS

Diagram 2-13

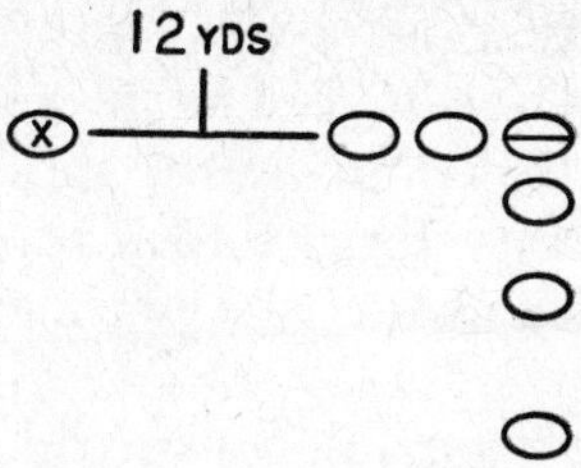

12 YDS

Diagram 2-14

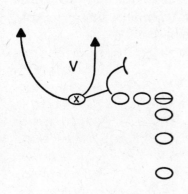

Diagram 2-15

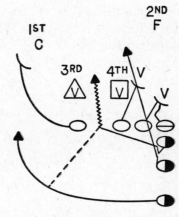

Diagram 2-16

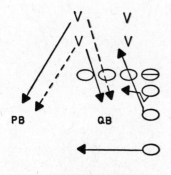

Diagram 2-17

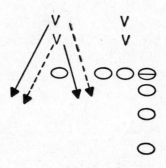

Diagram 2-18

for the TE (Diagram 2-19). The last alternative for the defense is to break down the stack and protect both outside and off tackle (Diagram 2-20). Forcing the defense to break down a stack is a strategic victory for the formationing concept. This breakdown completely eliminates the perimeter stunting game for stack defenses.

Aligning the TE in a spread position serves three important purposes: First, a three-deep secondary is stretched to a maximum. Diagram 2-21 illustrates a 5–3 defense. The spread formation forces this three-deep to be conscious of the entire field. This three-deep alignment is unable to rotate its coverage. The first defenders are isolated one-on-one with the TE and SE. This spread formation generally reduces the eight .man front by encouraging walkaway LBers to both sides. The first defenders, however, are still isolated with deep coverage responsibilities.

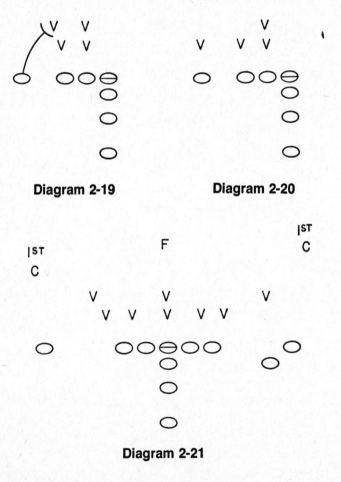

Diagram 2-19   Diagram 2-20

Diagram 2-21

Secondly, the spread formation forces a four-deep secondary to balance up (Diagram 2-22). The free safety is unable to become the fifth defender into the formation's strength on pitch-support or QB assignment. Diagram 2-23 illustrates the large middle zone created by an inverting free safety on option assignment.

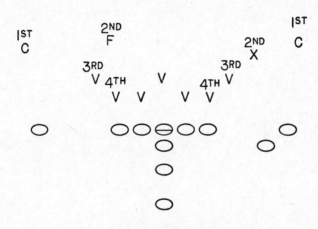

Diagram 2-22

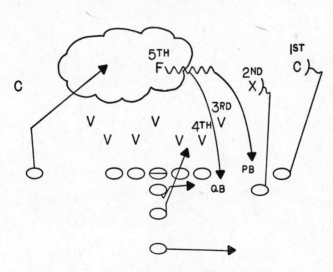

Diagram 2-23

Into the weak side of the formation, the TE's deep release prevents a corner roll to contain the pitch (Diagram 2-24). A weakside corner roll forces the free safety to cover tremendous territory. The TE becomes a pass threat when the corner commits to the LOS to contain the pitch. Should the secondary lock up in man coverage and invert the free safety into the weakside pitch-support (Diagram 2-25), the deep middle zone is susceptible to the play-action pass.

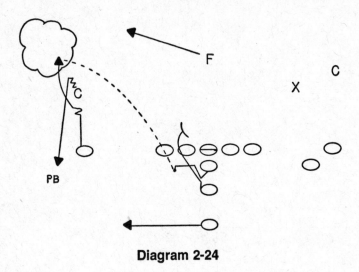

Diagram 2-24

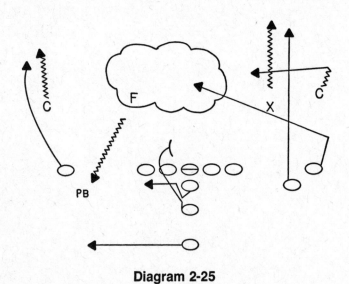

Diagram 2-25

The third advantage created by the spread TE is the inside blocking angle. Complementing option series, such as the lead option, can capitalize on the perimeter by cracking to the inside to seal off pitch-support and lead wide with the FB (Diagrams 2-26 and 2-27). The spread TE not only becomes a pass threat, but a perimeter blocker as well.

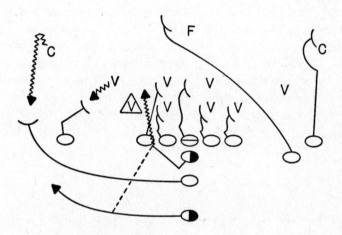

Diagram 2-26   Vs. 44 Stack

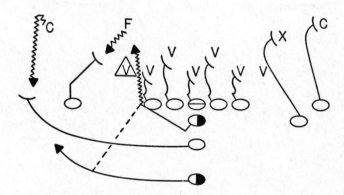

Diagram 2-27

The primary adjustment into the strong side of the formation is the slot alignment as diagramed in 2-28. Aligning Y in this position creates strongside blocking capabilities like those of the TE into the weakside of the formation. There are two ways to gain this strong blocking advantage. Aligning Y directly in the slot position is the first, and the second is to utilize Zip motion (Diagram 2-29).

Both Zip motion scheme and the slot formation contribute valuable strategic resolutions to the strongside formationing concept. First, this adjustment counters the effectiveness of a walkaway LB. Zip motion brings the third defender in closer to the formation. This defender is now positioned in an elucidated alignment (Diagram 2-30). Should the third defender elect to remain in a walkaway position (Diagram 2-31), the offense has gained two advantages. First, Y can release untouched into the secondary on a blocking or pass route assignment, and second, the QB's keep crease has been significantly enlarged. The fourth defender must now cover both the dive and the QB.

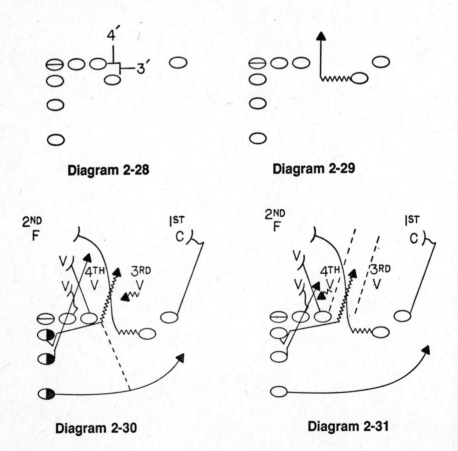

Diagram 2-28   Diagram 2-29

Diagram 2-30   Diagram 2-31

The slot alignment also generates an additional avenue to profit from talent placed at the slot position. Diagram 2-32 illustrates in part, Y functioning as the pitchback in the crazy option series. The weakside sprint-out pass series (Diagram 2-33) possibilities multiply and benefit by releasing Y into the secondary undisturbed and closer to the formation.

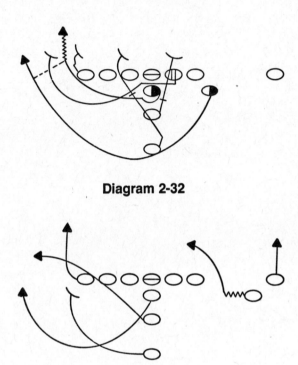

Diagram 2-32

Diagram 2-33

NUMBERING THE TWIN-I SERIES

The Twin-I multiple option series are numbered in intervals of tens. Numbering, rather than naming, each series shortens terminology in the huddle. A simple numbering system to describe each series is especially advantageous in audible and check-off situations on the LOS. Each of the Twin-I series has a specific backfield action which corresponds to a series identification number.

The Teen series (Diagram 2-34) is the *lead* option (sometimes referred to as the *speed* option). This double option quickly attacks the perimeter of the defense. Diagram 2-35 illustrates the counter dive to the FB and the counter double option are the core of the 20 series. The basic triple action (as diagramed in 2-36) is described as the 30 series. The crazy option or 40 series (Diagram 2-37) capitalizes with the TB counter trap and the crazy double option.

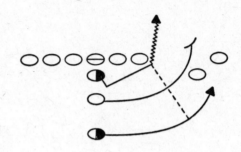

Diagram 2-34

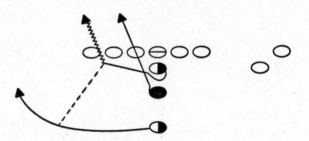

Diagram 2-35

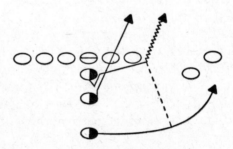

Diagram 2-36

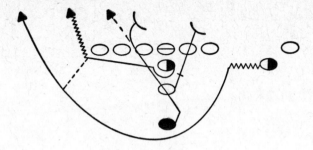

Diagram 2-37

Diagram 2-38 illustrates the 50 series or trap option action. Each of the five run series numbers also describes the blocking schemes to be employed.

The series identification number also describes the two basic passing series. The series number indicates the QB's setting action and the protection scheme. Diagram 2-39 illustrates the half-sprint set. The 70 series splits the backfield in the protection scheme. The 80 series, or full sprint (Diagram 2-40), assigns both backs to seal the perimeter, which allows the QB to break defensive contain.

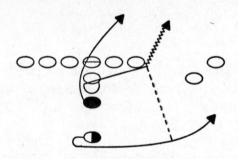

Diagram 2-38

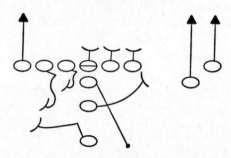

Diagram 2-39

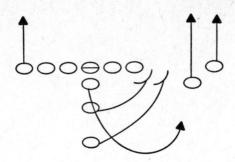

Diagram 2-40

Again, in a simple format are the Twin-I series:

Teen — Lead Option
20   — Counter Option
30   — Base Triple Option
40   — Crazy Option
50   — Trap Option
70   — Half-Sprint Pass
80   — Full-Sprint Pass

Each series is constructed with a double-digit number. The first identifies the series action, and the second designates the POA and the specific blocking scheme. An example is play "32." The "3" indicates triple option action. The "2" specifies the initial point of attack, which is the FB ride/decide over the right OG. "19" describes the lead option to the formation's left. "51" designates the trap option action with a FB trap at the "1" hole. Each series can be broken down to attack virtually every POA along the LOS. The flexibility of a series numbering system contributes to simpler play naming tactics.

The play-action pass series are three digit numbers. The series identifications number is added as a prefix. "3–32" indicates play action from the triple option action to the right side. Like the 70 and 80 series, play-action blocking schemes and pass patterns are taught in conjunction with the play number.

3

THE SELECTION
AND PLACEMENT
OF TWIN-I PERSONNEL

C oaching is personnel management. The ability to select and fit proper personnel into each offensive position is as critical as studying tactics, techniques, and the strategies of the game. Each offensive position carries with it criteria that will determine overall team effectiveness. There are specific requirements for each of the Twin-I positions. Each positional prerequisite is based solely upon the individual skill performance requirements.

This chapter discusses specific criteria for each offensive position. It is important to note that there is no mention of physical size. There are certain physical stature requirements that will be listed as helpful; however, the ultimate factor in personnel placement is dependent exclusively upon skill and assignment performance.

QUALIFYING THE INTERIOR LINE

Each position in the offensive line unit has assignment-related techniques that must be learned. Each of the three basic positions must be capable of mastering specific skills that relate to each phase of the multiple option scheme. The staffing of the interior line is often associated with generalities. The Twin-I systems assign specialized skill performance requirements for each basic interior line position.

The Center

More so than possibly any other interior position, it is helpful that the center possess two important physical attributes. Both physical characteristics focus on the center-QB ball exchange technique. The first helpful physical attribute is longer legs, and the second is a longer arm span.

Fitting the center to the QB is a critical issue. The QB's mobility is greatly affected by his pre-snap stance. Selecting a center with a high waistline complements the option QB's natural stance. A longer arm span aids the center's mechanics in two ways. First, the QB does not have to climb under the center to take the snap. A longer reach from center gives the QB vertical freedom to execute the FB mesh. Second, a longer arm span raises the center's balance point on the snap. His upper torso is able to move through a collision point rather than up to regain balance.

The Twin-I center must demonstrate the ability to execute three primary physical skills. The center must master an extremely quick snap. His snap must be consistently accurate in delivery and cadence. The center must demonstrate not only a quick snap, but quick movement off the LOS as well. Quick feet are a necessity to block the gap to either side. Snapping the ball and stepping through the playside gap is a concurrent assignment.

The center is a fulcrum position. All the option blocking schemes begin at this point and then develop toward the sideline. Therefore, the center must be capable of maintaining a square blocking base throughout the early stages of the option. Quick feet and hands are the two finest qualities an option center can possess.

The Guards

Selecting for the guard position is based exclusively on skill requirement. This position requires tremendous versatility. Primarily, the guards must be capable of controlling a single block on the LOS. Second, this position requires quickness for trapping, pulling, and fold blocking techniques.

The guards must demonstrate explosiveness from a stance into the LOS. The OG is not required to power defensive linemen away from the point of attack; however, an aggressive attitude is mandatory in neutralizing a defender beyond the LOS. The greatest assets a guard can have are a good, low center of gravity to facilitate movement into and along the LOS, and a desire to be effective as a single blocker.

The Tackles

Offensive tackles in the multiple option system play a unique role. The OT is selected for his ability to be flexible in technique execution. Primarily, the OT must be quick and evasive in releasing off the LOS. A big percentage of the OT's blocking assignments require downfield seal blocks on LBers. A high level of aggressiveness and ingenuity must be displayed if the OT is to be effective as a downfield blocker.

Directionally, the OT is required to execute not only a single block on the LOS, but to reach to the outside and at times to double down to the inside. It is critical that the OT be the most physical blocker on the LOS. Because of the diversity in his blocking assignments, the OT must be capable of neutralizing defensive containment outside of the OG-OT gap. His assignments include downfield, single, reach, double, and pass-blocking skills.

SELECTING THE PERIMETER CORPS

The perimeter corps consists of the TE, SLT, and SE. These three positions are selected to perform two primary assignments: blocking and receiving. To be successful, the option game depends upon the defense respecting the passing threat. The passing game is dependent upon an aggressive option attack to force the perimeter defenders to support the run. Both the run and the pass are interdependent. A collective prerequisite for the perimeter corps is to be an aggressive blocker and a consistent receiver.

The TE (X)

The TE can best be described as a mixture between an OT and SE. The TE must be physically strong to block inside and along the LOS. Yet, he must exhibit fleetness in downfield blocking and route execution. Physically, the TE must be durable. Releasing from the LOS under pressure and catching the short, quick passes over the middle require stamina and durability. The greatest asset a TE can have is open field agility. Blocking smaller, shifty defensive backs and running deep, isolated pass patterns requires good footwork and concentration. The TE is selected to fit into the Twin-I formationing philosophy. From a normal alignment, he is required to rub-double to the inside, single block, and release wide on the stalk block.

The TE is required to execute crack blocks from the flex and spread formations. His pass routes include short dumps, timing patterns, drags, and deep routes.

The Slot (Y)

The SLT position requires a blend between TE and SE techniques. The prime candidate for the SLT position is the individual who may not possess the physical strength to be an effective blocker in or along the LOS, or have the breakaway speed to be selected as the SE, but who has good downfield agility and pass-receiving skills. The SLT position requires an aggressive attitude toward crack blocking. Many option blocking schemes into the twin side of the formation require legal crack blocks.

There are two main attributes that complement the SLT position. The first is a quick release off the LOS into blocking schemes downfield. The majority of the defensive pitch support is targeted through the SLT area. The SLT must be an aggressive open field blocker. Second, the SLT must be a technician on timing pass routes. The timed outs, stops, and seam routes are a major part of the SLT's assignments.

The SE (Z)

The SE must be selected primarily for his receiving skills. This position is designated as the deep threat in the Twin-I package. Placing a receiver at this position who is a legitimate deep threat complements the perimeter blocking schemes. The SE must be effective as a stalk blocker; however, good speed commands defensive respect.

Three qualities a SE should have are:

1. The ability to be deceptive in changing his speed on his release from the LOS. This embellishes the play-action threat.
2. The SE must exhibit good concentration in catching the deep pass.
3. In addition, the SE must be effective as a runner after the reception.

SELECTING PERSONNEL FOR BACKFIELD POSITIONS

The I backfield positions are the QB, FB, and TB. Chapter 4 is dedicated exclusively to the selection and training of the option QB. Categorically, like the perimeter corps, the FB and TB harbor a dual role. These backfield positions are selected for their ability to both run and block.

The FB (3)

Prerequisites for qualifying as FB in the Twin-I system depend more on technical precision rather than physical stature. The following six criteria are used as guidelines in selecting the Twin-I FB.

1. The FB must be explosive in his start from stance. This explosiveness must be consistent. The QB/FB ride action is dependent on a constant mesh point.
2. Good ball control skills are mandatory. Covering the ball through the LOS is a specific skill that must be mastered to prevent fumbling or being stripped.
3. The FB must be deceptive into the LOS after the QB has disconnected.
4. Aggressive blocking skills at the perimeter are essential for effective pass protection.
5. The FB must be competent in receiving and running with short passes (i.e., screens, flats, and swing routes).
6. The FB must be physically durable.

The TB (2)

There are five primary qualities sought for in selecting the Twin-I TB. Foremost, the TB must be able to handle the pitch. Handling the quick or downfield pitch requires good concentration and peripheral coordination. Next, the TB must have sufficient speed and intuition to keep the constant pitch relation with the QB. Running and ball control skills require agility and quickness to utilize perimeter blocking schemes. In addition, the 40 series requires inside running skills. The basic blocking skills that are assigned to the TB demand aggressiveness in pass protection at the flank for both play-action and the open passing series.

4

DEVELOPING
THE OPTION
QUARTERBACK

The option QB in the Twin-I system is thought of primarily as a glorified HB who is a passing threat. No other single position carries with it more responsibilities and technique requirements than does the option QB. The success of this multiple option package is critically dependent upon the proper selection and development of the QB. However, basic option skills can be taught effectively to personnel that normally qualify as QB material.

CHARACTERISTICS OF THE OPTION QB

The primary physical attribute the option QB must possess is that of durability. The nature of this position requires an aggressive desire to advance the football during development of the option. The option QB must surrender to the fact that physical contact comes with the position. Any hesitation toward challenging defenders defeats fundamental option objectives. The QB must be physically competent to be a legitimate running threat.

There are five skills that the option QB must demonstrate competency in, or the potential to develop.

1. Quick hands and feet are essential in working along the LOS. Controlling the football requires dexterity. Executing each phase of the option demands exactness in training. Adroitness is imperative in skill performance.

2. Quick reaction to visual stimuli is manifested through good hand-eye-foot coordination. The option QB functions in a reacting position. Good agility and physical-visual coordination are critical prerequisites.

3. To be effective as a ball carrier, the QB must exhibit good speed. Functional speed begins at a 4.8 time in the 40-yard sprint. Speed is analyzed in two fashions. The first is acceleration from a stance, and the second is breakaway capabilities.

    Attacking each option point along the LOS is dependent upon quick acceleration on the snap. The need for the QB to pressure the defense immediately is unavoidable. Quick acceleration from a stance is essential. Breakaway speed is a luxury. Open field running skills can replace the lack of possible breakaway speed.

4. Running skills are self-evident in the Twin-I QB selection process. The expectation held for the FB and TB in relation to possession and ball control are relevant to the QB.

5. The final skill, not often associated with option packages, is the ability to develop as a passer. Passing the football is not a luxury—it is a necessity. The Twin-I QB's ability to pass competitively creates a new dimension in the multiple option system.

In addition to physical and skill prerequisites, three specific character traits are cultured. The Twin-I QB must be a student of the game. Successful game planning is dependent upon practical knowledge exhibited through performance. The QB must be willing to accept the leadership role associated with this position. Considerable time must be sacrificed for technique development. Finally, the QB must take pride in developing a purist attitude toward technique practice and execution.

COACHING THE QB'S OPTION TECHNIQUES

The primary phase in instructing the QB in optioning techniques is done in conjunction with the offensive center, then progressing on with the FB, then adding the TB. It is imperative that this early technique phase be rehearsed without defensive reads or keys of any type. Each phase of the option is predetermined. Breaking down each phase into separate technique actions facilitates troubleshooting. This prepares the QB for the transition into the reading and optioning cycle. Two separate sequences are incorporated to teach the option techniques. First is the option core, and second is the option point sequence.

The Option Core Sequence

This teaching phase polishes the core option techniques involving the center, QB, and FB. Each step is described in detail, then systematically drilled as a unit.

Taking the Snap

The QB assumes a balanced toe-to-toe stance behind the center. The knees should be slightly bent to form a natural squat position. The shoulders are kept parallel to the LOS. The arms are extended under the center with the top hand following the middle seam of the center's pants. The elbows are slightly flexed to keep the QB's shoulders relaxed and limber. The bottom hand pressures the top hand through the heel of the palm. The fingers are hyperextended in a reaching fashion.

The exchange is made on cadence by the QB lifting with the bottom hand giving the center a strong pressure target. The bottom fingers curl around the belly of the ball and top fingers over the laces. The ball is withdrawn into the QB's stomach. Simultaneously, the QB steps back to the FB mesh point with the playside foot.

Coaching Points:

1. The QB's pressure target should be sufficient to force the center to take a forward balance step.
2. The heels of the QB's palms should not separate during the exchange. Firm pressure with the bottom hand eliminates exchange fumbles.
3. The QB must settle the ball into his "third hand" (lower sternum), before extending toward the FB mesh. This prevents swinging the ball into a collision course with the FB.

The Mesh

As previously mentioned, the QB takes the snap from the center while simultaneously stepping to the mesh. Stepping with the playside foot at 4:00, the QB plants as deep in the backfield as possible. His hips should be parallel to the sideline. The ball is extended from the "third hand" toward the far hip of the FB. The ball is rotated forward, placing its long axis parallel to the ground. The mesh is completed once the QB is able to apply pressure with the back of his inside hand to the FB's abdomen.

Coaching Points:

1. The ball is gently placed in the QB's soft folding pouch—not slammed. The mesh is a smooth interreaction.
2. Once the ball is meshed, the QB's inside elbow should be slightly flexed. His lead arm is fully extended to keep the ball in place during the ride. A full extension of the lead arm places the mesh at a maximum depth.
3. The actual mesh is made with the QB's peripheral vision. The QB must concentrate on keeping his chin over the lead shoulder, focusing on the LOS, rather than watching the FB mesh.

The Ride

The QB's ride with the FB is actually made on one foot. The QB's playside step plants firmly at the mesh point. His offside foot is adducted to regain balance, then extended toward the LOS. Diagram 4-1 illustrates the "J" or ride step executed by the offside foot.

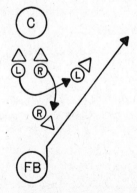

Diagram 4-1

The purpose for this "J" step is threefold. First, the step allows a deeper FB mesh, which gives the QB more reading time while moving toward the LOS. Second, the step removes the QB away from possible penetration through the center-OG gap. Third, the depth provided by the step puts the QB in a position to attack downhill toward the option point.

Coaching Points:

1. The ride step is relatively short. A half step toward the LOS keeps the QB positioned for his downhill angle after the disconnect from the FB. Overstriding jams the FB into the LOS and prevents the QB from continuing down the path.

2. Once the mesh is initiated, the QB must not crowd the FB's dive path. The QB's hips must be kept parallel to the sideline. The QB's arms should glide uninhibited toward the LOS during the ride step. The ride should appear as if the QB were sliding the football smoothly across a waist-high table top at arm's length.

3. To prevent the QB from being dragged through the LOS by the FB, the football must be given or disconnected by the time the ride step is planted. A QB rule on the ride is: "never ride past your belt buckle."

4. The ball must be kept parallel to the ground on its long axis. Tipping either end up binds the football inside the FB's pouch should there be an attempt to disconnect.

The Give

Once the mesh is nestled in the FB's pouch, the QB's fingers should extend lengthwise over the belly of the ball. The give is made by withdrawing the inside hand against the FB's stomach while applying decisive pressure with the lead hand.

Coaching Points:

1. The QB's inside hand must be withdrawn completely to clear the FB's hip. Dragging the inside hand congests the QB's movement down the LOS behind the FB.

2. The QB must consciously avoid watching the FB into LOS. Both the eyes and action must carry out the option fake.

The Disconnect

The disconnect is made by spreading the QB's elbows and drawing the ball back to the third hand. Flexing the elbows wide prevents the FB from clinching the ball away from the QB.

Coaching Points:

1. The ball must be withdrawn on its parallel axis. The ball will catch in the FB's inside arm if the nose is up.

2. The ball must be rotated back into the third hand as the QB steps in behind the diving FB. Bringing the ball back to the sternum protects against fumbling during the disconnect and prepares the QB for the option point sequence.

The Core Drill

After each separate technique in the core sequence is explained and rehearsed, actual drilling begins. The core drill is the first phase in working the complete unit. Diagrams 4-2 and 4-3 illustrate the layout for this drill. Traffic cones are set one yard off the LOS simulating the outside hip of the OG. The coach aligns two yards outside the traffic cone on the LOS to observe the drill development.

Drill Objective: To teach the predetermined give and disconnect techniques; to introduce the fundamental option timing between the center, QB, and FB; to develop the QB's confidence in the meshing and ride action.

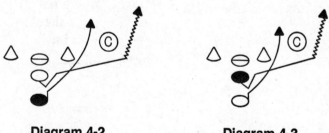

Diagram 4-2   **Diagram 4-3**

Drill Procedure: First, the predetermined give is rehearsed (Diagram 4-2). A full cadence is used to simulate a true game situation. Next, the predetermined disconnect is practiced (Diagram 4-3). Last, the coach calls out either "Give" or "Disconnect." It is imperative that this phase be totally mastered before adding the pitchback or defensive reads.

Coaching Points:

1. The QB's eyes should be focused on the coach through the drill procedure.
2. After the give to the FB, a good outside keep fake is rehearsed (Diagram 4-2).
3. On the disconnect, the QB polishes the keep technique (Diagram 4-3).
4. The QB is taught to explode behind the FB downhill regardless of giving or disconnecting.
5. An effective variation in installing confidence in the mesh and ride with the FB is to blindfold the QB. Blindfolding the QB quickly identifies any weakness in the core sequence.

The Option Point Sequence

The option point sequence exclusively polishes the keep or pitch techniques after a predetermined disconnect from the FB. The TB is added in this drilling sequence. The primary concept the QB must master prior to keeping or pitching the football is the correct downhill attack angle after disconnecting from the FB. The inside hip of the defender at the OP must be rapidly attacked. Moving parallel to the LOS or bowing away allows the OP defender to string out or delay the keep/pitch read. Diagram 4-4 points out the correct downhill angle the QB must pursue to force an immediate commitment from the OP defender.

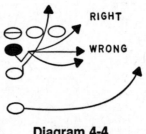

Diagram 4-4

The Keep

Keeping the football requires an assertive attitude by the QB. The QB must expect contact beyond the LOS. However, his running style should reflect a cautious and intelligent demeanor.

Coaching Points:

1. All fakes at the OP are done with two hands on the football. A one-handed fake pitch is asking for a fumble. Head fakes or change of pace fakes are much safer and more effective.

2. The QB must square his hips to the goal line immediately after dipping into the LOS. Failure to do so forces the QB to veer toward the sideline, nullifying any downfield pitch to the trailing PB.

3. The QB must be conscious of keeping the ball covered with both hands. Only after the keep breaks into the secondary should the ball be tucked outside into running form.

The Pitch

The final technique in the OP sequence is the pitch. There are currently two philosophies in executing the pitch. The first is the "push pitch," similar to a basketball set shot. The second is the "wrist flick" that forces the thumb down and away from the body. There is nothing sacred about either style; either one can be effective. Smaller hands that cannot grip the football as securely gain control from the push pitch. Larger hands that feel comfortable with the wrist flick can get the pitch off faster. Fitting the type of pitch to the QB's physical capabilities is the key to selecting the pitch style. In either case, there are several points that are universal.

Coaching Points:

1. The pitch must be taken from the sternum directly through the downfield shoulder. Pitching above the shoulder hangs the ball in mid-air. Pitching lower than the shoulder (i.e., off the hip) drops the ball at the PB's feet.

2. The pitch must lead the TB in his arc route. A short step and look at the OP by the QB minimizes poor or uncontrollable pitches.

3. After the pitch is released, the QB must not relax. Most defenses assign a defender to collision the QB each time the option develops. Contact is generally made at the instant of the pitch or slightly after. Bracing for contact after the pitch is a measure of self-preservation.

The "OP" Drill

The OP drill polishes only the predetermined keep or pitch techniques. Diagram 4-5 depicts the organizational scheme for the OP drill. After disconnecting from the FB, the QB executes either predetermined technique as assigned. Every possible situation is set up prior to the snap. The keep, the quick pitch, and the delayed downfield pitch are all rehearsed during the OP drill.

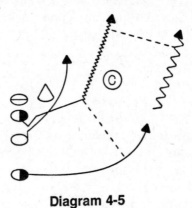

Diagram 4-5

Coaching Point:

Along with the keep/pitch techniques, the coach should observe the mesh, ride, and disconnect techniques. Appropriate option fakes are demanded throughout the OP sequence.

The "Pre-D" Drill

This drill consists of the complete option action with no defensive reads. The same format is extended from the "OP" drill. However, each phase of the complete option action is predetermined. The Pre-D drill is the final technique phase that must be mastered prior to installing the thought process and inserting defensive reads.

A good, strong, quick and accurate pitch technique can be developed. The following are two specialized drills that concentrate exclusively on the pitch technique.

The Triangle Pitch Drill

Three QBs align in a seven-yard balanced triangle. Only one ball is used during the drill (Diagram 4-6). Each QB receives the pitch, then settles the ball into a firm set position at the sternum. The QB buzzes the feet momentarily to simulate attacking the OP, then steps and pitches to the next QB. The QB's eyes should focus on the coach in the center until the moment of the pitch. This drill strengthens the nondominant arm by emphasizing pitching through the lead shoulder.

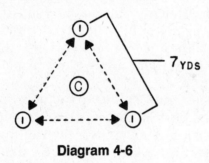

Diagram 4-6

The "CC" Pitch Drill

The "cross-country" pitch drill is illustrated in Diagram 4-7. Two QB's are aligned seven yards apart on the sideline facing across the field. The first buzzes his feet and steps through on the

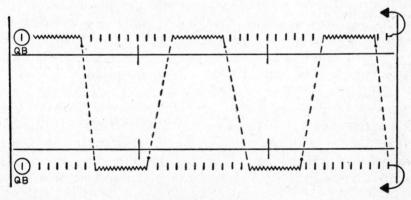

Diagram 4-7

pitch to the second QB. Immediately after pitching the ball, the first QB sprints to create a correct pitch angle. After three or four pitches across the field, the pair turns back, which develops the pitch with the opposite arm.

TRAINING THE OPTION THOUGHT PROCESS

The QB must be armed with a specific response for each of the dive and keep/pitch reads prior to the snap of the ball. The thought process establishes a specific priority at each read point along the LOS before the actual decision must be made. A predetermined thought process gives the QB a solid blueprint from which sudden decisions can rationally be made. When specific rules are given to the QB from which the option sequence can be developed, "and if" situations are eliminated from the teaching and drilling procedure. The option QB will be much more effective and aggressive if he knows exactly what he is going to do prior to the snap. The QB need only to react to defensive intentions that challenge the pre-determined blueprint.

Teaching phase one of the thought process involves the center, the QB, and the FB. The ride/decide thought process is the fundamental of triple optioning. As the QB approaches the center, his thought process is: "I will give to the FB—unless I read disconnect." The QB's first intention is to give to the FB on the dive. Knowing this, the QB need only disconnect when the dive is taken away. Only two reads are taught to the QB that signal disconnect. The first is a pre-snap read, the second is a post-snap read.

The pre-snap read identifies defensive alignment that eliminates the fourth defender as the dive-read. Diagram 4-8 illustrates the fourth defender reduced down into the OG-OT gap. This alignment threatens to force the QB deep into the backfield off his downhill action. This fourth defender must be sealed from penetrating or feathering laterally. A pre-snap read of this alignment automatically reduces the triple to a double option.

The only post-snap read for disconnect that the QB must learn is when the fourth defender commits directly to the FB. This ride/decide is illustrated in Diagram 4-9. The fourth defender has committed to a collision point with the FB. The QB rides to his belt buckle, then disconnects and attacks downhill. Any other techniques used by the fourth defender are not absorbed. Should the

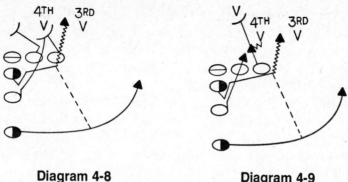

Diagram 4-8   Diagram 4-9

fourth defender *squat,* or step out and then back to game the QB, is immaterial. Giving the ball inside against an unconventional defender will soon condition a collision response. The QB need not be confused by a mishmash of "and if" read criteria. A single pre- and post-snap read accurately determines the dive's chances of success.

The ride/decide drill is illustrated in Diagram 4-10. The core drill format is used to rehearse the QB's thought process and subsequent technique execution. The coach aligns in the fourth defender's position. It is imperative that during the early stages of this drill, the QB is told exactly what direction the fourth defender will take. The thought process is then associated with the expected response. Gradually, as the QB gains confidence in his reading ability, the thought process alone governs a cat-mouse game between the fourth defender and the QB.

Phase two of the option thought process is rehearsed with the TB included. The QB's thought process after disconnecting from the FB is: "I will keep—unless I read pitch." The QB's second intention is to keep the football. This aggressive attitude forces the

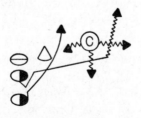

Diagram 4-10

third defender to commit quickly to his option assignment. The QB will develop into a running threat once he grasps the realization that he is not a liaison between the FB dive and the TB pitch, but a designated ball carrier. Only two defensive reads are associated with pitching the football. The first is the committed third defender and the second is the boxed read.

The committed defender is defined as one whose assignment or intention is to tackle the QB on or behind the LOS. Diagram 4-11 depicts a patience defender who tackles the QB only after waiting to be approached. On the turnside, Diagram 4-12 illustrates a crashing defender whose intention is to collision the QB as deep in the backfield as possible. Both of these defenders are assigned to prevent the QB keep; therefore, the response to the thought process results in the pitch.

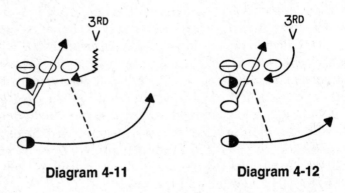

Diagram 4-11   Diagram 4-12

The boxing end is the only other read that results in a pitch. If the third defender squares up to the QB, the QB must "walk up in his face" and pitch the ball. The defender that turns his back to the sideline cannot possibly cover both the QB and the FB. The QB can lead the PB far outside the option point by walking up into the boxing end's face and pitching the football (Diagram 4-13). Any other techniques used by the third defender (i.e., *feathering*, slowplaying, or gaming) are ignored. The OP defender, like the fourth defender, can be conditioned to respond. Keeping the QB's reads simple is far more productive than isolating every possible defensive read.

The keep pitch drill is a double option drill that rehearses the QB's second thought process (Diagram 4-14). Like the ride/decide drill, the coach aligns in the third defender's position. The QB is instructed to disconnect from the FB and attack the OP. Also like the aforementioned drill, the QB is informed as to the intentions of

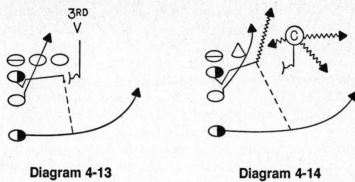

Diagram 4-13   Diagram 4-14

the third defender. Developing the thought process is relative to confidence gains. After significant practice, the third defender's intentions are read exclusively via the thought process.

Phase three in the teaching sequence is the combination of the full backfield versus the third and fourth defenders (Diagram 4-15). The "Option Drill" incorporates the full thought process with technique execution. The third and fourth defenders are role-played by the next FB and TB to run the drill. The coach aligns behind the TB out of the QB's vision. By using hand signals, each defender is given a predetermined response. On the snap, the QB executes the complete triple. Trouble-shooting is easy since the coach is aware of the option outcome. As the QB gains confidence in the basic triple reads, more complex defensive alignments are substituted into the drill.

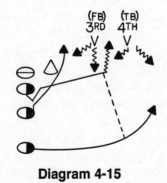

Diagram 4-15

DEVELOPING AN EFFECTIVE PASSING TECHNIQUE

Passing techniques, like optioning mechanics, can be isolated and rehearsed to a degree of functional effectiveness. Understanding the mechanics of passing a football is as critical as understanding fundamental option techniques. Great passers, like option QB's, are not born—they are developed.

The first criterion that must be isolated in developing an effective passing technique is the QB's natural throwing rhythm. Each QB's style is unique to his size and kinesthetic structure. Polishing the rough edges off a natural throwing action is more profitable than the mass overhauling of a passing style. Passing styles cannot be cloned. Each must be developed within the framework of its natural capabilities. Each passing style must subscribe, however, to four intrinsic components that when incorporated, improve upon the overall passing mechanics. The four checkpoints, or components for developing an effective passing technique are: the grip, the release, the follow-through, and the passing stance or set position.

The final outcome in the pass flight pattern is dependent upon the grip on the football. The grip is the actual launch point; therefore, a good passing style begins with a good grip.

The third and fourth fingers overlap the laces on the back one-half of the ball. The thumb is wrapped around the football, where it applies firm pressure opposite the overlapped fingers. The index finger is spread toward the tip of the ball. The small finger counters the index finger's pressure through the long axis. The grip should be firm and comfortable while not restricting the natural circumduction of the wrist. Tightening the spiral on the pass is dependent upon the index finger position and the wrist flick action during the release. A comfortable grip promotes confidence in controlling the football. The following isometric drills develop grip strength and coordination.

The "Thumbs-Down" drill is a primary strengthening drill. Two QBs grip the top belly of the football. The arms are extended and the ball is raised to shoulder height. The object of this drill is to rotate the thumb down and under (simulating the wrist flick release), while twisting the football out of the opposing QB's hand.

The "End for End" drill requires the same two QBs to grip the football at the ends, placing the tip into the pit of the palm. All five fingers should extend lengthwise toward the laces. The arms are completely extended and the ball is raised again to shoulder height. The object of this drill is to draw the football away from the opposing QB by flexing the elbow. The ball should not be turned or twisted to gain an advantage.

The release is made directly above the passing arm shoulder. The arm is near full extension with the wrist cocked back to keep the tip of the football up. The index finger last touches the ball as the thumb rotates down and away from the body midline. The release is accented by a quick downward flick of the wrist. A general rule in troubleshooting to tighten the spiral on the pass is to spread the index fingers closer to the tip of the ball and develop a quick, crisp wrist flick on the release.

The follow-through is an expression of a correct passing form. The passing action must be channeled into a natural and smooth rhythm. Upon the release of the ball, the passing arm continues down in a natural motion toward the opposite knee. During the early stages of training, the young QB is required to gently tap the opposite knee as a reminder to correctly follow through.

The QB's opposite arm is used as a counter force to proliferate maximum torso rotation. Once the football is raised into a release motion, the opposite elbow is driven back and away from the throwing direction. This component of the follow-through squares the shoulders and generates maximum strength into the release.

The release and the follow-through are separate components in the passing motion but are drilled concurrently. Both are inter-related; therefore, drills are designed to develop the complete sequence. The "Wall" drill is the primary teaching tool. The QB is positioned with his feet toe-to-toe, firmly planted fifteen feet from the wall. The objective of this drill is to develop a strong torso rotating action and to teach a nose-up, high release on the football. A spot is placed on the wall at shoulder height for focusing purposes. If the QB is releasing the ball properly (assuming the QB is right-handed), with the nose slightly elevated, the clockwise spiral on the ball will cause the football to bounce off to the right side or directly back to the QB. Should the wrist not be sufficiently cocked, the nose will tip downward, causing a sharp rebound to the left. The wall drill is designed to isolate on the upper torso throwing mechanics. The feet are kept firmly planted to prevent the hips from engaging into the throwing action. This drill serves as an excellent warm-up and self-check drill prior to all throwing sessions.

The "Net" drill emphasizes the complete throwing motion. Two QBs are placed on opposite sides and ends of a tightly stretched volleyball net. The QB's throwing arm is kept into the net. The net is strung to the QB's standing reach height. The objective of this drill is to force the QBs into adopting a straight-over-the-shoulder high release as a component of their passing style.

Each QB, in turn, raises up on the balls of his feet and steps through the complete passing action. The ball is zipped over the net to the opposing QB's outside breast. The proximity of the net forces a high release and a natural rotating follow-through.

The "Hot Potato" drill teaches the QB to find the laces and quickly release the football in good passing form. Two QBs face each other in the open field. Eight or ten footballs are placed on the ground several feet from the first QB. The coach or manager kneels down and flips each football in rapid succession to the QB. This drill requires the QB to concentrate on perfecting his grip and quickly delivering the football to the appointed target. The second QB gathers the footballs at his feet as he makes each reception. The drill is repeated in the opposite direction.

It is important to teach the QB to focus on a specific target during each of the preceding drills. Stressing the concept of focusing on a small target improves passing accuracy. A spot is marked for the Wall Drill. The target for the Net and Hot Potato drills rotates in a clockwise fashion from the opposing QB's breasts, to his forehead, and then to each hip. When the QB focuses on the receiver as a general target, the ball is likely to be thrown in the general area of the receiver. Once the QB focuses on a specific part of the receiver, for example the outside hip, the ball, in all probability, will be confined to a more condensed area around the targeted hip.

The passing stance or set position is the foundation from which the passing action is built. The hips are cocked squarely facing the target. The ball is secured over the strong arm breast en route to the high release. The chin and chest are up in a balanced position. The pass's initial power is generated from the hips. Therefore, the knees are slightly flexed, anticipating the hip thrust to begin the passing motion. This basic set position is drilled for the majority of the play-action series and the complete 70 or half-sprint series.

The play-action drill is illustrated in Diagram 4-16. Three receivers are added to the core drill format. Fundamental mesh and ride techniques are stressed along with a three- and five-step setting depth.

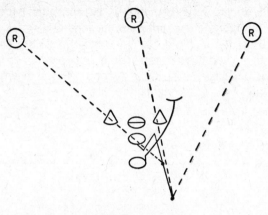

Diagram 4-16

Coaching Points:

1. Patience is stressed during the run-action fake. Effective play-action passing depends upon good run-action fakes. The QB is the key to creating a first-class fake. Keeping the eyes on the LOS and riding the FB to the belt buckle require a commitment to patience.
2. Upon the disconnect from the FB, this drill stresses an explosive retreat to launch point.
3. Once in the set position, the shoulders and hips are squared to the LOS. The feet are kept alive in a quick buzzing action until the football is released.

The 70 series setting drill (Diagram 4-17) rehearses the QB's half-sprint passing stance. The QB takes the snap, then opens with the onside foot at 4:00. The three-step is for the quick pass routes, the five- and seven-step depths are for medium and deep pass patterns. The QBs set and pass to the opposite receiver. The ball is then rotated forward to keep the cycle going. The QBs exchange positions to polish the setting action to both the right and left side.

Coaching Points:

1. The QBs are given different focus points on the receivers. The inside breast is relative to the post pattern strike point. The outside hip is for the out routes and the navel is for the curl route.

2. Specific setting times are drilled as minimum expectations. These set times are defined as the time consumed from the snap exchange until the QB is in his set position. This timing does not include the release. The five-step set is drilled in 1.7 seconds, the seven-step in 2.0 seconds. These minimum standards teach the QB to hustle into his set position.
3. Like the play-action drill, the QBs are required to buzz their feet up through the release. Dead feet reduce the QB's mobility during the passing play.

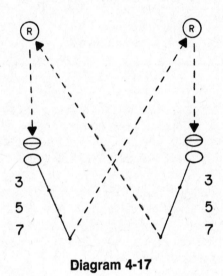

Diagram 4-17

The 80 series drill (Diagram 4-18) schools the QB in throwing on the run upon breaking outside contain. The QBs rotate through this drilling sequence by passing to the inside receiver, then retrieving their own pass on their way to the next center. A maximum number of passes can be thrown via this rotating drill in a short period of time.

Coaching Points:
1. The QB takes his first step at 6:00. The depth of the sprint action is determined by the depth of the receiver's route. The QB should reach the maximum sprint depth behind the OT. A six-yard depth is standard for shorter timed routes while a nine-yard retreat facilitates deeper throwback or delay routes.

2. During the sprint action, the QB must be prepared to deliver the pass anytime after breaking the OT alignment. The QB's throwing action on the sprint must be natural and continuous. The ball is released at the top of the throwing arc.

3. The mistake most often made by young QBs is to overstride on the release. Doing so reduces both the hip and torso flexibility. This loss in flexibility diminishes both the power and accuracy of the pass.

4. Lastly, the QB must be cautioned against throwing across his body. The shoulders and hips must squarely attack the LOS during the passing motion. Maximum passing efficiency is dependent upon correct technique. The passing motion must be a continuation of the sprint direction. Throwing across, rather than with, the body destroys proper technique.

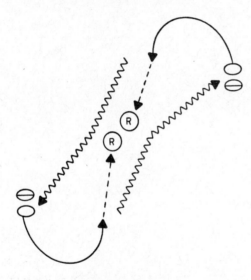

Diagram 4-18

COACHING THE QB'S GAME INTELLIGENCE

Option QBs are placed in a very responsible position for technique execution, as this chapter has detailed. Following the mechanics of optioning and passing comes the application stage. This stage is manifested through the QB's game intelligence. Game intelligence refers to the functional and practical execution of rehearsed techniques. *Making things happen* is possibly more decisive phraseology. Since the QB is the catalyst, his knowledge of defenses that have been designed to stop the option is imperative. Along with counting defenders to each side of the formation to determine general strengths, the QB must be drilled to recognize expected defensive fronts along possible option defending schemes.

Each anticipated defensive front is drawn on a 5″ × 7″ card (Diagram 4-19a). These cards detail the option defense schemes that are most likely to be seen. The next cards (Diagram 4-19b) are extracted from scouting report data. Subordinate defensive adjustments represent stunting or gaming alignments. These cards are arranged by down and distance.

It is virtually impossible to eliminate all surprise situations during the course of a game. However, the more prepared the QB is in recognizing traditional defensing schemes, the more effective his interpretation skills will become.

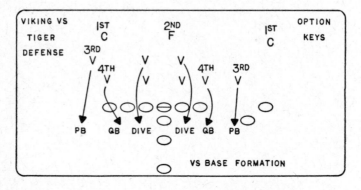

Diagram 4-19a   Viking Vs. Tiger Defense Option Keys

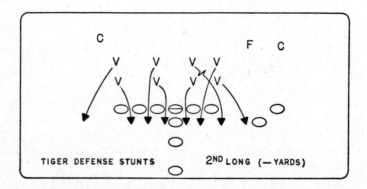

Diagram 4-19b   Tiger Defense Stunts

5

INSTALLING
THE TRIPLE OPTION
SERIES

T he foundation of the Twin-I multiple option system stems from the basic 30 or triple option series. The option concepts learned from the basic play 32/33 can be applied into each of the complementary option series. This basic triple option play is the driving force behind fundamental offensive game planning. Defenses must be convinced to respect 32/33 in their game planning alignment.

DEFINING THE TRIPLE OPTION ASSIGNMENTS

The complete assignments for 32/33 are outlined as follows (Diagrams 5-1 and 5-2):

Center: Over backside LB through the playside gap. (The playside gap concept will be discussed in Chapter 6.)

On Guard: #1 outside breast through the playside gap.

On Tackle: First LBer over, or to the inside. Take the safest release to LB.

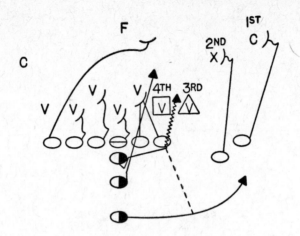

Diagram 5-1   Vs. 52 Defense

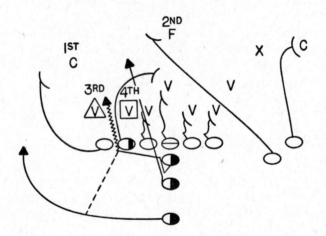

Diagram 5-2   Vs. 43 Defense

Coaching Point:

The On Tackle's release must be quick and clean. He cannot be delayed by the DT. Diagram 5-1 illustrates an inside release versus an outside shade defender. When this defender is aligned head up or inside, the OT must quick-step around to the LB (Diagram 5-2).

Off Guard: #1 inside breast through the playside gap.

Off Tackle: #2 inside breast through the playside gap.

TE: Onside—outside slow arc block on first defender.
Offside—inside release, stalk block deep safety.

SE: Onside—stalk block the outside breast of the first defender.
Offside—stalk block inside hip of first defender. Prevent the defender from flowing playside.

SLT: Onside—stalk block the outside breast of second defender.
Offside—stalk block the deep safety across the field.

FB: Mesh step with the playside foot. Landmark the outside hip of the On Guard. Soft fold over the ball reading the QB's give or disconnect signal.

TB: Open to the sideline with a playside step. Sprint toward the sideline keeping a 4×4 yard pitch relation with the QB. Always expect a quick pitch. Use a limp arm technique in receiving the pitch.

QB: Open and mesh with the FB while reading the fourth defender to initiate the triple option. The thought process is, "I will give to the FB unless I read disconnect." After the give, carry out the option fake down the LOS. Should the read be "disconnect," attack downhill to the option point. The thought process is, "I will keep unless I read pitch."

INSTRUCTING BACKFIELD OPTION TECHNIQUES

The QB's option techniques have been previously detailed in Chapter 4. The remaining FB and TB techniques tie in the completed triple option play. Each has specific positional techniques that, when blended together, embellish a smooth development of the basic 32/33 play. Since this play is taught in a core sequence, each of the backfield positions is interrelated. Therefore, each position must consider his own role performance as the most important faction within the play.

The FB

The FB is coached to assume a balanced toe-to-toe three-point stance. The three-point stance was selected over the four-point stance for a number of reasons. The three-point stance gives the FB more flexibility for lateral movement. Arc blocking on the perimeter and pass blocking at the flank both require a direct approach. The four-point stance is too restrictive. The three-point stance is more versatile with respect to both the dive action and lateral movement.

Teaching the FB to mesh properly with the QB on the basic option ride reduces exchange fumbles and technical errors during the ride/decide. The most important component of the FB's dive technique is the initial mesh step. Diagram 5-3 illustrates the short twelve-inch step taught to the I FB. The mesh step is a short forward jab step taken with the playside foot. This step directs the FB toward the mesh point. The QB does not have to overextend to hook up for the ride. The QB is able to place the ball deep inside the FB's pouch. The FB's second step is directly at the OG landmark. The propinquity of the mesh step aligns the dive path with the QB's reach. A direct step to the OG's outside hip forces the QB too deep. The ball is not secure on the FB's inside hip. The dive develops into a belly or arc course.

On the mesh step, the FB elevates the inside elbow to accept the QB's reach. The inside arm softly folds over the QB's extended arms. The outside arm cups under the ball with the palm up. The elbow is spread slightly away from the body. This serves as a stopping point should the ball be overextended through the pouch.

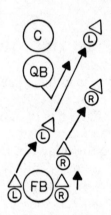

Diagram 5-3

Coaching Points:

1. The FB is coached to dive hard and low. His knees should drive high and quick through the LOS.
2. When the FB interprets the give, both hands close over the tips of the ball. The ball is completely covered until the FB breaks into the secondary.

3. When the FB interprets disconnect, the shoulders must be squared to simulate the give. The FB continues through on the dive fake looking to draw tacklers or cut off pursuing LBers. It is imperative that the FB dive through the LOS. Stopping after the disconnect prevents the QB from working beyond the FB ride.

The TB

The TB is taught to assume a semi-erect two-point stance. The feet are comfortably spread to near shoulder width. The head is up, shoulders squared, with the palms of the hands lightly placed in the hip crease. The TB's weight should be evenly distributed over the balls of both feet. A "credit card" should be able to be slipped under the TB's heels. This balanced stance facilitates quick movement forward or laterally in either direction.

On the snap of the ball, the TB's initial reaction is a playside step directly toward the sideline. The TB must aggressively sprint the "seven-yard highway" toward the sideline. As the TB pivots toward the pitch route he must always expect a quick pitch. This awareness concept keeps the TB conscious of his 4×4 yard pitch relation with the QB.

Coaching Points:

1. The TB is instructed to use a limp arm technique while running the pitch route. The inside arm is kept relaxed and limp. This limp technique allows a quick reaction to gather the low or behind-the-shoulder pitch. A rigid, driving inside arm cannot scoop up an off-target pitch.

2. The pitch-receiving technique is taught in conjunction with the limp arm. The pitch is received by extending the inside arm and cupping the football back into the body. The inside arm acts in a similar fashion as a shock absorber. The ball is controlled with the outside hand as it is quickly shifted into the outside arm.

3. Once the pitch is secured, the TB is coached to "milk the sideline" for maximum yards before looking for a cutback route. All perimeter blocking schemes are designed to break the pitch-back down the sideline.

Drilling the Option

Three independent drills are utilized to introduce the option unit to live game situations. The first drill in this controlled scrimmage sequence is the "Interior drill."

The interior drill format pits the offensive line and backfield versus the core defense minus its secondary (Diagram 5-4). The objective of this drill is to polish the basic 32/33 optioning techniques in conjunction with both the on- and offside blocking schemes. Both the offensive and defensive units operate from out of a huddle. A complete cadence and audible system is used to simulate live scrimmage situations.

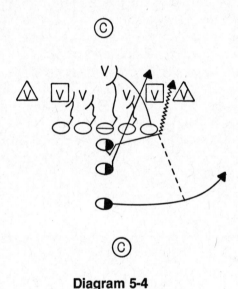

Diagram 5-4

Coaching Point:

The defensive unit is instructed to execute stunts and/or alignment shifts in specified sequences. The object of this drill is to familiarize the offense with the stunts and games that will be encountered. Drilling situations should not be designed to confuse the offense. Each drill should promote confidence and clarity in the optioning process.

Once the interior line and backfield gain confidence in the timing and techniques for 32/33, the receivers are added into a half-line situation. The onside assignments are emphasized in the half-line drill. The objective of this drill is to allow each side of the offensive line to work the onside assignments with both the SLT and SE (Diagram 5-5) and the TE (Diagram 5-6). The backfield is introduced to defensive schemes on both sides of the formation. The receivers now develop their stalk block timing on the perimeter.

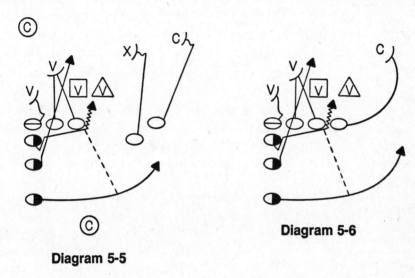

Diagram 5-6

Diagram 5-5

Coaching Points:

1. With the receivers added to this drill, complete defensive schemes are used against the option. However, each scheme is introduced to the offense in a teaching situation, then promptly drilled.
2. Both the offensive and defensive units operate from out of the huddle. The TE and SE/SLT alternate turns in the huddle. This sequence allows maximum drilling in a short period of time.

The final drill in this sequence is the option drill. The complete offensive unit is confronted with a full defense in a scrimmage situation. Down and distance situations are created. Defensive tendencies are correlated with each down. The offensive unit is limited to the basic triple play. Correct execution and assignment recognition is crucial since the defense is aware of the intended offensive play.

Coaching Points:

1. The only alternate weapon allowed the offense is an audible to change the direction of 32/33 at the LOS.
2. The defense is encouraged to play honest in alignment and technique. The purpose of the drill is to polish the complete triple option; not to establish a dominance or rivalry.

COACHING THE SPECIAL PROBLEMS

There are several defensive alignments that break all the option rules and assignments. These exceptions to the basic rules are labeled as special reads or problems. Once these alignments are learned and recognized, traditional option objectives can be applied.

The Gap 8 defense is illustrated in Diagram 5-7. This defense is designed to penetrate through each gap along the LOS so that it applies immediate pressure to each phase of the option. The offensive line splits are reduced to a minimal distance to counter this defensive objective. When playing versus the Gap 8 front, all interior linemen are assigned to block down on the defender in the gap. The center's rule requires him to block through the playside gap. The interior gaps are sealed from penetration, leaving the third and fourth defenders isolated in optioning positions.

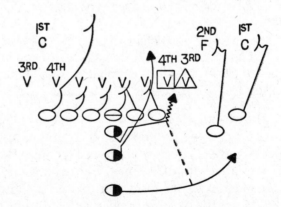

Diagram 5-7   Vs. Gap 8

The QB's primary rule for a pre-snap read would require an automatic disconnect from the FB. However, identifying the Gap 8 as a special read, the QB makes the adjustment to the fourth defender as the dive-read. The FB is able to see the gap alignment and to adjust his dive path outside of the OT's down block. The triple option as the basic play now has a good chance for succeeding.

One of the biggest problems faced by triple option teams is the stacked defense at the option point. Stacks present difficult read problems for the QB. In some cases, the stack completely destroys the mechanics of the QB's thought process. Therefore, rather than complicate the QB's rules and thought processes, the stacked defenses are designated as special reads. Diagram 5-8 illustrates a stacked 5–3 front. The gapped DT normally indicates a predetermined disconnect from the FB for the QB. The stacks at the option point can stunt in or out and confuse the QB's decision process. This alignment does in fact destroy the standard option process.

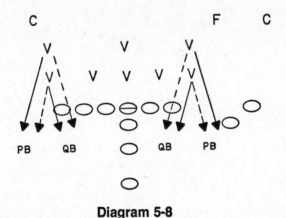

Diagram 5-8

The Twin-I triple option directly attacks the stack with the FB and the ride/decide. In most stacks, the defender on the LOS is the fourth man, the dive-read. Therefore, the interior blocking schemes are adjusted to seal off everything to the inside of the stack (Diagram 5-9). Once the stack is isolated, the QB's thought process still applies. The first intention is to give on the FB dive. The stack is read as a unit, rather than individually. The QB is drilled on reading the reaction of the stack. Diagram 5-10 illustrates a 44 stack defense in a game situation. With repeated drilling, the QB can

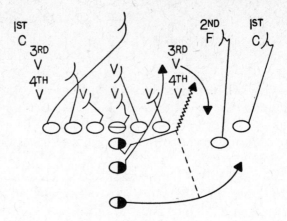

Diagram 5-9

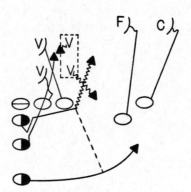

Diagram 5-10

determine which defender is responsible for the FB. The ride/ decide is far enough away from the stack so that the defense must commit quickly on their assignments. Once the stack declares its intention, the QB focuses on the defender who has been assigned to close off the inside. A key note of emphasis is that the defender who has been assigned to the inside can be directed at either the FB (to stop the dive), or the QB (to force the pitch). However, this defender cannot cover both the FB and the QB. Therefore, the QB is coached to key this defender's eyes. The stunting defender's eyes will give away his intended collision point. Should this defender close on the FB, the QB disconnects and carries out the second phase of the option.

The twin receiver alignment is susceptible to a unique defensive alignment not often faced by other option formations. The walkaway LB aligned over the SLT presents a special problem for the triple option. The split 60 defense with a walkaway (Diagram 5-11) assigns the DT to attack the FB from the inside-out. The DE forces the immediate pitch while the walkaway LB comes up on pitch-support. The first priority in optioning the eight-man front with a walkaway is to locate the fourth defender and seal everything off to the inside.

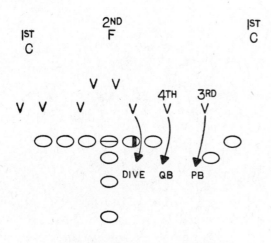

Diagram 5-11   Vs. Split 60

The fourth defender is isolated in Diagram 5-12. A fold blocking scheme is used to seal off the DT's collision course. It is futile to assign the SLT to stalk block a walkaway so close to the LOS. Open field blocks are sufficiently difficult without having to maintain one indefinitely on the LOS. Therefore, the third defender is left in an optioning position. The FB is directed slightly under in his dive path. The fourth defender is now forced to decide between the FB or the QB. In reality, this defensive alignment reduces the triple to a give/keep double option. The TB rarely sees the pitch when a defender such as the walkaway LB is assigned to collision the TB's pitch route at the snap of the ball. The fourth defender must be accurately read. The option has little chance of succeeding if the fourth defender intimidates the QB and forces both the disconnect and the pitch. The walkaway alignment spreads the defensive front. The fundamental thought process sequence is valid once the fourth defender is isolated.

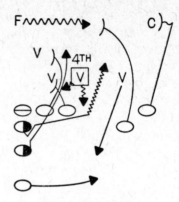

Diagram 5-12

WINNING VARIATIONS WITHIN
THE TRIPLE OPTION SERIES

The Twin-I multiple option system is structured around the basic triple option play. However, 32/33 is only one variation in the complete 30 series package. Defenses encountered are structured primarily to stop the triple option. Therefore, variations of 32/33 blend effectively into the 30 series assignments and techniques. The initial triple option backfield action conditions defenses to react to their option assignments. The four primary variations that fit into the option disguise are: the hard dive, the double option, the cutback dive, and the outside veer.

Play 34/35

Play 34/35 is the hard dive within the 30 series. The hard dive is incorporated for three primary reasons. First, to attack directly at weak defensive personnel. Second, to take advantage of defensive design such as a deep bubble over the OT in the 43 college front (Diagram 5-13). Thirdly, the hard dive quickly capitalizes on over-pursuing LBers. Diagram 5-14 depicts the inside LBer scrapping quickly to the outside in pursuit of his QB assignment. Many defenses become vulnerable to the hard dive simply because they are coached to outnumber the option at the perimeter.

The assignments for 34/35 are designed to simulate the triple option action.

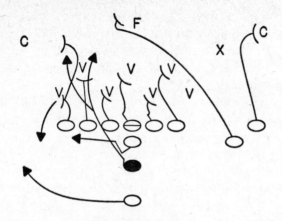

Diagram 5-13

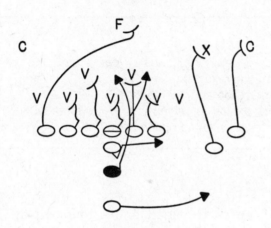

Diagram 5-14

Center:	Over, backside LBer through the playside gap.
On Guard:	#1 outside breast. Drive through the defender, maintaining maximum contact. If #1 is a LBer and takes a side, lock on and drive him in the direction he is going.
On Tackle:	#2 inside breast. Aggressively seal off any inside movement by the defender. Should #2 be a LBer, work into his numbers and drive him in the direction he wants to go.
Off Guard:	#1 inside breast through the playside gap.
Off Tackle:	#2 inside breast through the playside gap.

TE:	Onside—#3 inside breast. If #3 releases to the outside, continue downfield for first defender (Diagram 5-13). Offside—inside release to block the deep safety.
SLT:	Onside—stalk block the inside breast of the second defender. Offside—inside release to block the deep safety.
SE:	Stalk block the first defender's inside breast.
FB:	Take the playside mesh step and receive the ball. Ride into the LOS keying the On Guard's block. Read daylight once the exchange is final.
TB:	Explode on the pitch route carrying out the option fake.
QB:	This is a predetermined give to the FB. Ride the FB into the LOS, give the ball and carry out the option fake. Do not look back to the FB, keep the eyes down the LOS.

Coaching Point:

The QB can draw defensive pursuit by carrying out the option fake. The keys to a good fake are:

    a. a smooth ride and give to the FB;

    b. a quick explosion behind the FB down the LOS;

    c. eye contact with the option point.

Play 38/39

The 30 series predetermined double option is play 38/39. The advantage of including the double option into the triple option package is correlated with the defensive option assignments. The first example is evident when a defense assigns the DT to crash inside to shut down the dive. Allowing this collision with the FB slows down the QB's approach to the option point. Therefore, the double option assigns the On Tackle to drive block the DT (Diagram 5-15). The FB becomes an additional blocker to seal off pursuit toward the perimeter. The QB is now able to disconnect freely from the FB and quickly attack downhill to the option point. Play 38/39 pressures the perimeter immediately with the QB keep or pitch.

The assignments for 38/39 are illustrated on Diagrams 5-16 (versus an even 4–3) and 5-17 (versus an odd 5–2).

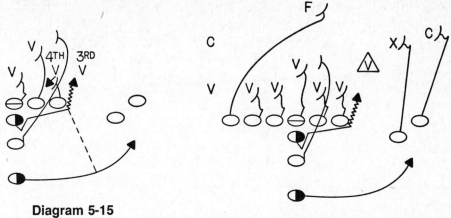

Diagram 5-15

Diagram 5-16

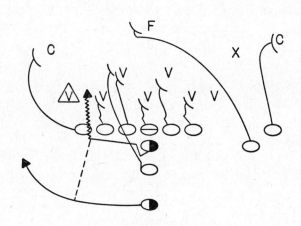

Diagram 5-17

Center:	Over, backside LBer through the playside gap.
On Guard:	#1 outside breast.
On Tackle:	#2 outside breast. Attack the outside breast directly to prevent the defender from pursuing laterally to block to the outside. Maintain maximum blocking time.
Off Guard:	#1 inside breast through the playside gap.
Off Tackle:	#2 inside breast through the playside gap.
TE:	Onside—outside release and slow arc block the first defender.
	Offside—inside release and block the deep safety.

SLT: Onside—stalk block the second defender's outside breast.
            Offside—inside release and block the deep safety.

SE: Onside—stalk block the first defender's outside breast.
            Offside—drive the first defender deep.

FB: Mesh step and ride through the LOS. Explode into any
            pursuing defender. Execute a good dive fake to draw
            defensive attention.

TB: Pitch route, expect a quick pitch.

QB: Disconnect from the FB and attack the option point. The
            thought process is: "I will keep, unless I read pitch."

Coaching Point:

Since the QB does not have the dive read, he can evaluate the option
point before the snap. The QB can observe possible stunting alignments that eventually will affect the optioning thought process.

Play 30/31

   The cutback dive is the first misdirection play that comes off
the basic triple option action. Play 30/31 is exclusively used to dive
the FB back underneath overpursuing LBers. Diagram 5-18 illustrates the FB slipping out the backdoor versus a 4–3 defensive
front. The straight-ahead diving action is confusing to defenders
who have been coached to pursue toward the option flow. The
cutback dive attacks quickly and directly at the heart of every
defensive front.

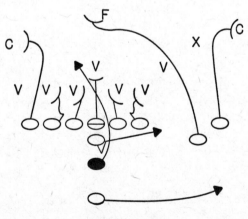

Diagram 5-18

The basic assignments for 30/31 are outlined below.

Center:	Over, onside LB through the playside gap. The center's block must be aggressive. The FB's cutback is directed behind the center's blocking direction.
On Guard:	#1 inside breast through the playside gap.
On Tackle:	#2 inside breast through the playside gap.
Off Guard:	#1 inside breast through the playside gap.
Off Tackle:	#2 inside breast through the playside gap.
TE:	Inside release and stalk block the first defender's inside breast.
SLT:	Inside release to block the deep safety.
SE:	Stalk block the first defender's inside breast.
FB:	Landmark the center's playside hip. Take a straight-ahead mesh step, key daylight off the center's block. The cutback seams open up radically back to the offside.
TB:	Carry out the pitchback fake.
QB:	Open deep at 6:00. Mesh and ride the FB straight ahead. After the give, explode down the LOS carrying out the option fake.

Play 36/37

One of the most popular variations to the triple option currently marketed is the outside veer. The outside veer adds a unique dimension to the triple package that confuses and disorganizes option defending assignments. The primary function of play 36/37 is to move the triple option one hole wider along the LOS. The third defender is isolated as the dive-read and the first defender is attacked as the option point is read (Diagram 5-19). The TE is assigned to assist in sealing off the fourth defender en route to cutting off inside LBer pursuit. Defenses must incorporate alternate option assignments to include the outside veer threat.

The split backfield has claimed a dominant role in executing the outside veer. Most literature credits the split backfield as the absolute "best" from which an outside veer can be successfully run. This is not necessarily true. The dive back in the splitback alignment declares his dive path immediately on the snap. Defenses can adjust their option assignments by reading the blocking pattern of the TE and the diveback's initial movement (Diagram 5-20). The outside veer is an effective play from the splitback alignment. However, the I formation multiple option package creates unique

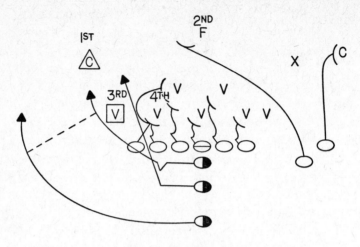

Diagram 5-19

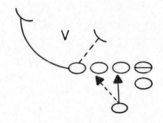

Diagram 5-20

advantages with the outside veer that are not possible from the split backfield.

The primary advantage created by the I formation is that of disguise. The blocking pattern and the initial backfield action is identical to the lead option series. Defenses are unable to detect any variance in the play development. The outside veer from the I formation is more likely to see standard option defensive techniques at the read point rather than adjustments designed exclusively for the split backfield. Slow playing, feathering, or boxing ends are very vulnerable to the I formation outside veer.

The split backfield alignment is susceptible to encounter hard crashing ends that are assigned to collision the QB/FB mesh, which in turn forces the option to accelerate. The "sink" end is another popular technique to counter the splitback outside veer (Diagram 5-21). The third defender aligns one yard off the LOS and reads the TE's helmet. When the TE releases inside to block the outside veer, the DE is assigned to attack the dive back as deep in the

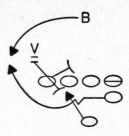

Diagram 5-21

backfield as possible. This forces the QB off his downhill approach and stretches the option out. The inside LBer keys the diveback's directional step. He is assigned the QB on the outside veer scheme. When the TE releases outside to stalk block for the inside veer, the DE is assigned to wait for the QB and force the pitch. The inside LB is a secondary support on the QB after checking the inside veer. The splitback alignment declares the inside and outside veer too quickly. The I formation is less likely to see these complicated defensive schemes designed especially for the outside veer since this play is only a variation play, rather than a core option scheme.

The assignments for play 36/37 versus a 4–3 front are shown in Diagram 5-22:

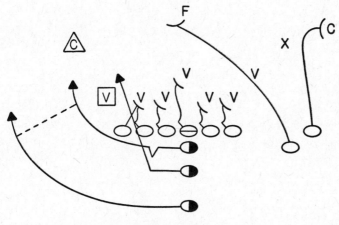

Diagram 5-22

Center: Over, backside LB through the outside breast. The TE will rub-double down to help secure the block. Both the hips and shoulders must drive straight upfield to keep the DT from pursuing toward the outside.

Off Guard:	#1 inside breast through the playside gap.
Off Tackle:	#2 inside breast through the playside gap.
TE:	Seal off first LBer to the inside. If the OT is covered by a down lineman, rub-double with the OT to secure his block. Slip off to block the first inside LBer.
SLT:	Inside release and block deep safety.
SE:	Drive the first defender deep.
FB:	Open laterally with the playside foot. Plant the third step firmly and landmark the outside hip of the On Tackle. Mesh with the QB on the fourth step and read the give/disconnect pressure.
TB:	Pitch route. Keep a proper pitch relation with the QB outside on the perimeter.
QB:	Open directly down the LOS with the playside foot. Step back and mesh with the FB on the third step. The thought process is identical to play 32/33. The basic triple option mechanics apply throughout the play. Should the read be "disconnect," quickly turn the corner and attack the first defender's inside hip. Keep the pitch possibility alive as far downfield as possible.

6

EXPLOSIVE BLOCKING TECHNIQUES FOR THE TWIN-I TRIPLE OPTION

Blocking schemes and techniques for the Twin-I triple option package differ greatly from traditional power or sweep teams and even somewhat from current option systems. There is also a philosophical difference in that the Twin-I option blocking patterns are designed for succinct execution and finesse. In a system such as the triple option, where timing and exactness are paramount, raw power schemes are not a prerequisite to create openings along the LOS. Designed blocking patterns that create an offensive advantage in conjunction with simple blocking techniques is the core objective of the Twin-I triple option.

There are three primary objectives that are uniformly effective in teaching Twin-I triple option blocking techniques. The first is a quick explosion from the stance. Getting movement off the LOS is imperative. The surge from the LOS is crucial in creating the proper downhill attack angle for the QB. Second, an aggressive blocking style must be adopted. Each blocker is convinced his block will spring the big play. Effective blocking is 50 percent technique and 50 percent attitude; therefore, staying with a block is an issue of pride as well as skill. Thirdly, each blocker will develop the skills to neutralize defenders across the LOS. The key difference with regard to other technique philosophies is that of neutralizing rather than powering or forcibly dominating defenders. The Twin-I philosophy is designed to prevent defensive flow toward the playside.

DEFINING 30 SERIES INTERIOR BASE BLOCKING TECHNIQUES

There are two basic blocking philosophies that are prevalent in current option blocking schemes. The first is zone or area blocking, and the second is a man assignment. The Twin-I system subscribes to the man assignment philosophy. The basic block for the interior five linemen that complements this philosophy is the single or drive block. There are five components of the drive block that when isolated and drilled separately facilitate teaching the overall objectives of option blocking. The components are: stance, playside step, target point, contact, and follow-through.

The Stance

"A good block begins from a good stance" is an irrefutable cliché. With this in mind, the stance selected for the interior line should parallel their anticipated technique requirements. Two basic stances are taught in Twin-I interior line; a four-point for the center, and a three-point for the remaining four linemen.

The center assumes a balanced four-point stance with the body weight distributed over the balls of his feet. The ball is gripped over the laces with the thumb and offset slightly outside the center's vertical plane. The opposite of the balanced hand is placed on the ground with the fingers extended to complete the balanced four-point stance. The center's head is raised far enough to keep the back relatively parallel to the ground. The knees are slightly bent to ensure flexibility for lateral movement. Once the weight is properly distributed, there should be "air" under the center's heels. This balanced four-point stance facilitates a natural snap and step rhythm. Since the center is required primarily to work through the playside gap en route to his assignment, a natural four-point stance is very serviceable.

The remaining offensive linemen are coached to assume a heel-to-toe three-point stance. The body weight is distributed over the power or up foot, and the back or balance foot. The down hand is lightly placed on the ground to square the shoulders and to support the final stance. The opposite arm lightly rests over the power knee. The forehead is slightly up and the chest is somewhat parallel to the ground. If the stance is balanced, the down hand can be swung free between the legs without disturbing the overall stance balance.

This balanced stance is used to expand each lineman's mobility. Alternate option schemes and complementary series utilize pulling and trapping techniques along the LOS. This versatile stance permits aggressive drive blocking as well as pass protection techniques. A primary key in developing the interior stance is to adjust each stance to the physical stature of the athlete. The stance must complement the natural movement. In adapting each position into a stance, two cautions are observed. First, the bunched or toe-to-toe stance is awkward. Forward movement is highly restricted. The second is the elongated stance. Forward motion is improved, but lateral movement is forfeited. The balanced stance is by far more productive with regard to technique and skill requirements.

The Playside Step

The success of the triple option is contingent upon sealing off defensive pursuit toward the option flow. The first priority of the offensive lineman assigned to a specific numbered defender is to protect the playside gap. The offensive line as a unit is drilled to anticipate defensive slanting or stunts through each playside gap. Therefore, with the exception of the Onside Tackle, who is assigned to seal either the LB over or to the inside, the first step off the LOS is a 45° playside positioning step into the onside gap (Diagram 6-1). This first step does not alter the lineman's upfield surge. The shoulders and hips are squared to the goal line. The playside step is a quick jab that protects the near gap from defensive penetration.

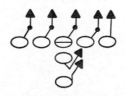

Diagram 6-1

Even though the Twin-I system subscribes to man blocking as its primary rule, the playside gap concept borrows from the zone philosophy. As Diagram 6-2 illustrates versus a 44 stack inside stunt, the man assignments become flexible when onside gaps are threatened. The center's rules are "over backside LB through the playside gap." There is no defender over, so therefore the backside LB is targeted. However, the playside gap is the foremost assignment and the stunting LB is threatening to penetrate the onside gap. The center must first secure this gap before moving on with the assignment. The onside tackle's assignment stunts away, therefore he continues through, anticipating flow toward the playside. All stunting and slanting into the playside can be neutralized through this concept. The initial jab step and check quickly sets in motion the fundamental drive block.

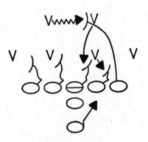

Diagram 6-2

The Target Point

The term "inside or outside breast" is repeatedly used in blocking assignments. The objective of the drive block is to penetrate into the defender's body. A defender cannot be effectively neutralized without making contact with the body frame. The defender's breast is isolated as the primary contact point for the blocker's face mask. The primary objective of the target is give the blocker a collision point. If the breast is attacked properly, the blocker's hat slips off to the playside and the shoulder absorbs the contact. The blocking position is low, balanced, strong, and legal. If the blocker is facing a down lineman, the breast is the gateway into the defender's hips. Against a defender in a two-point stance, the breast as a target facilitates proper positioning into the playside without sacrificing balance or drive strength.

The Contact

The actual collision with the defender is paramount in the overall structure of the drive block. It is the initial contact that stuns the defender's charge and initiates playside gap control. First contact is made with the face mask to the target point. Follow-up contact immediately ensues with a *forearm lift.*

The forearm lift is the primary weapon that each blocker must develop. The upper cut collision from the lift elevates and neutralizes the defensive charge. The mechanics of the lift require that the forearm be kept parallel to the body from the belt line up through full shoulder extension. The lift is a quick ripping motion that draws its momentum from the initial hip thrust out of the stance. Good lift action is crucial to generating the proper drive action up through the defender.

The forearm lift is taught in a three-step progression. First the blocker is placed kneeling erect with both fists clenched at the belt buckle. A large cylinder dummy is held one foot in front of him with the top tilted forward to lightly touch the blocker's hat. On the command, the blocker rips up through the dummy with a forearm lift, then quickly resets.

Coaching Points:

1. The lift is initiated from the belt line. The blocker must not wind up by drawing his forearm behind his back. The lift is a short, quick upper cut.

2. At this point, the blocker is taught to "sky the eyes." The head is thrust up and back in conjunction with the lift. This coordinated movement prepares the blocker to keep his head up during the final teaching stages of the drive block and to generate maximum hip thrust from the three-point stance.

The second step in the progression emphasizes the importance of the hip thrust. The blocker is placed on his hands and knees (six-point stance) in front of an air bag that is held upright at his shoulder level. On command, the blocker lunges forward, ripping upward with the prescribed forearm. The eyes are skied to force the back to hyperextend. The opposite arm is driven past the air bag to cushion the blocker's fall to the ground. The blocker quickly resets in preparation to continue the drill.

Points:

1. The quick forward lunge from the six-point stance should force the face mask and forearm to simultaneously strike the air bag.
2. If the lift is executed properly, the blocker's hips will touch the ground first, followed by the opposite hand and finally the chest.
3. The power in the lift must now be generated in the hips and transferred through the thrust into the forearm lift.

The final step in the teaching progression links leg power into the collective thrust and lift action. The blocker is aligned in his proper stance in front of a large cylinder dummy. The bag is held two feet in front of him, with the top tilted forward to about a half foot in front of the blocker. The bag is tilted to give the blocker a solid surface with which to make contact. On the cadence, the blocker explodes from his stance up through the bag into full extension. This phase does not require the blocker to step into the bag. The completed extension and lift forces the blocker to land belly first on to the ground. The head should be up, the opposite arm completely extended beyond the bag, and the forearm lifted high above the head in full extension.

> Coaching Point:
>
> This step in the forearm lift teaching sequence is crucial in developing the explosiveness off the LOS that is necessary in option blocking schemes. The drill is designed to be simplistic in technique rehearsal while allowing maximum repetition during the drilling sequence.

The Follow-Through

Once the initial contact has been made, the follow-through techniques are the crux of the block. To complete an effective drive block, six elements of the follow-through must be observed.

1. First, the blocker must localize his power into the defender's hip area. The objective of the drive block is to get into and pressure the defender's hips. The defender is at a strength disadvantage when he is forced above the offensive blocker. The defender's hips are a solid blocking surface and must be aggressively attacked to neutralize the pursuit.

2. The blocker's hips and shoulders must be squared to the goal line throughout the duration of the block. The thurst off the LOS and the playside step perpetuate the correct upfield movement. The FB's dive crease is protected and defensive flow into the perimeter is neutralized more efficiently by a uniform upfield surge rather than by stepping and stalemating on the LOS.

3. The opposite or playside hand is driven beyond the defender to the ground. The driving action is supported on three points. Keeping the opposite hand on the ground forces the blocker to stay low and use the legs for power. This low profile prevents lunging at the defender.

4. The blocker's head must be kept up. This promotes visual contact and also broadens the blocking surface of the shoulder and forearm. Pressure is applied through the shoulder and forearm surface after the initial contact is made. A wide V-shaped blocking surface is created by raising the head up in conjunction with the forearm lift. The defender's movement can be controlled with head and forearm manipulation.

5. Once contact is made with the defender, short chopping steps are used to keep the drive block pressure constant. Elongated lunging steps cause the blocker to lose the broad-based balance that is necessary to maintain power throughout the block. Short, quick driving steps generate consistent and uniform power in the block.

6. The final component of the follow-through is the time element of sustaining contact. The average play time lasts between 4.5 and 4.6 seconds. Therefore, the drive block is drilled in 6.0-second intervals. It is important to establish this concept of maintaining the block as long as possible Drilling in 6-second intervals establishes the proper precedent for executing the drive block. Maintaining proper blocking position requires mental commitment as well as the technical requirements.

DRILLS FOR TEACHING THE DRIVE BLOCK

After the fundamental forearm lift has been learned, the following drill sequence is used to teach the drive block in its entirety.

The Board Drill (Diagram 6-3)

Equipment: One 10' × 1' board and one tall cylinder dummy.
Objectives: 1. To develop a wide base for the drive block.
2. To teach a sustained driving action for the six full counts.

Method: The dummy is held on one end of the board. The blocker
                aligns slightly to one side of the bag and two feet away. On
                the cadence, the blocker explodes into the bag via the
                playside step. The head is driven through the playside of
                the bag. The bag is driven the length of the board.

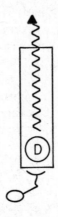

Diagram 6-3

Coaching Points:

1. The bag is held with firm resistance to simulate defensive pressure.
2. Initial contact is made up through the bag. The opposite or
   playside hand must be in contact with the ground to keep the
   block low and balanced.
3. Short, quick steps are emphasized to drive the bag the length of
   the board.
4. The blockers alternate sides to work both the right and left
   playside step.

The Chute and Bag Drill (Diagram 6-4)

Equipment: One blocking chute and one tall cylinder dummy.
Objectives: 1. To teach the blocker to come off the ball low.
                2. To emphasize a low wide base from the stance to block a
                   defender aligned off the LOS.
Method: The dummy is held two feet beyond the chute. The blocker
                is aligned directly over one leg of the chute. On the ca-

dence, the blocker drives up through the chute making contact with the bag. The block is maintained for the six counts.

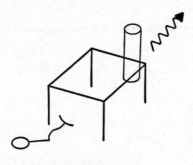

Diagram 6-4

Coaching Points:

1. The blocker must be taught to keep his base under the chutes by dropping his hips rather than by ducking his head.
2. The blocker must run through the bag rather than dive into the block. A wide base and balance is critical for effective drive blocking.

Zig-Zag Drill (Diagram 6-5)

Equipment: One tall cylinder or square dummy.
Objective: 1. To teach proper weight distribution to the opposite hand during the drive.
              2. To promote hip flexibility and coordination while driving a moving target.
Method: The blocker is slightly offset in front of the tall dummy. On cadence, the blocker drives into the bag and executes the proper playside step. The defender holding the bag retreats in a "Z" pattern. The blocker maintains contact and position throughout the drill.

Coaching Point:

The blocker's hips and shoulders must be kept parallel to the goal line. The blocker moves in unison with the zig-zag action.

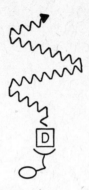

Diagram 6-5

Sled Drill (Diagram 6-6)

Equipment: One seven- or three-man sled.
Objective: To develop a uniform surge by the complete line from cadence.
Method: Slightly offset a blocker over each station along the sled. On cadence, the unit surges into the sled, driving through the six-second count. The unit must come off the ball and make contact together if the sled is to be driven evenly.

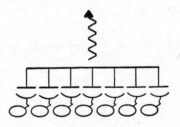

Diagram 6-6

Coaching Point:

A key point of emphasis is the use of short chopping steps to drive the sled. Long lunging strides lose the driving power.

Lover's Lane Drill (Diagram 6-7)

Equipment: Two large dummies laid on the ground five yards apart from boundaries.

Objective: To place a blocker and a ball carrier in a controlled scrimmage situation versus a live defender.

Method: The blocker and the defender are aligned head-on inside the boundaries. The coach stands behind the defender and signals the playside to both the blocker and the BC. On cadence, the blocker explodes into the playside breast of the defender. The BC attacks the playside gap. The drill is concluded upon the BC breaking through the boundary or being tackled.

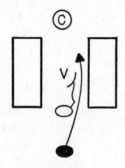

Diagram 6-7

Coaching Point:

This one-on-one drill isolates on all the fundamentals that appear in the drive block. A point of emphasis is that the block cannot be stalemated inside the boundary. The upfield surge is a key factor in the drive block.

TEACHING PERIMETER BASE BLOCKING

The basic block used to break down perimeter defenders is the stalk block. Unlike the interior blocking techniques, the stalk block is an open field block that requires unique skills and techniques.

However, perimeter blocking parallels the interior assignments in that an aggressive attitude toward blocking is cultured. Any open field block is difficult at best, but fine tuning the specific techniques along with the correct attitude results in effective stalk blocking. A standard rule for the Twin-I perimeter corps is: "No blocks, no biscuits." The passing and running games are so heavily interrelated that the perimeter corps must develop equal attitudes toward pass receiving and blocking. A primary reason for developing the great stalk block is evident in the design of the basic option play. The long run down the sideline by the pitchback is launched by an effective downfield block.

There are five elements of an effective stalk block: the stance, the release, the drive, the breaking down, and collisioning. Each of the perimeter positions will vary in different elements of the stalk block. However, the fundamental stalk blocking techniques are prevalent.

The Stance

The two fundamental stances taught in the perimeter corps are a single stance for the SE and SLT, and a combination stance for the TE.

The SE and SLT share a common elongated three-point stance. The outside leg is back and the corresponding hand is down. Regardless of the side of the center where these two receivers align, the outside leg is back for step-counting on specific, timed pass routes. The inside arm is extended back to rest lightly on the hip pad. This gives the receiver a clear visual line to the ball. The elongated sprinter's stance permits the receivers to accelerate immediately off the LOS.

The TE is coached to use a more balanced heel-to-toe three-point stance similar to those used by the interior linemen. The TE is required to release inside or laterally to the outside to avoid contact. The three-point stance is also better suited for the blocking assignments in and along the LOS. This balanced stance accommodates the TE's technique requirements from his normal alignment. From the spread formation, the TE is required to use the same elongated stance as prescribed for the SE and SLT.

The Release

There are four objectives in teaching the outside release for the triple option:

1. Foremost, it is vital that the blocker gain an outside leverage on the defender. The option is designed to break the pitch up the sideline.

2. By releasing outside, the defender is forced to turn his back away from the developing play. This destroys defensive option keys for pitch support.

3. The outside release gives the receiver a deep takeoff route up the field if his release is not respected.

4. The outside release is consistent for evading immediate defensive pressure (i.e., LBers, walkaways, and bump coverage).

The SE release is designed to get maximum horizontal and vertical stretch in the secondary. The SE aims for an imaginary spot two yards wide of the first defender. This wide release insures the proper positioning into the defender's outside breast (Diagram 6-8). If this defender is to maintain correct coverage position, he must widen and deepen with the SE's release.

The SLT release is very critical because the majority of defensive pitch coverage is designed to invert through the SLT position. Therefore, the SLT is not afforded the luxury of a wide release to gain a tactical advantage. The SLT's target spot is the outside hip of the second defender. An outside advantage is gained, but more importantly, should the second defender commit up to the pitch, the SLT is in line to block beyond the LOS (Diagram 6-8).

The TE's release is referred to as a "slow arc" (Diagram 6-8). Keeping his hips squared upfield, the TE opens laterally to gain an outside position on the first defender. The TE attacks upfield as he

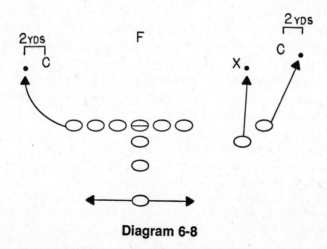

Diagram 6-8

gains the outside two-yard position. The result is an arc-shaped release path. The TE must follow the same wide release rules as the SE when he is aligned in the spread or flex formation. The TE, like the SLT, must expect a quick defensive commitment up to support the pitch. The slow arc gives the TE a good view of defensive pitch coverage.

The Drive

All three positions share a common purpose in this phase of the stalk block. The most dangerous key that a receiver can give to his defensive counterpart is that of a difference in his driving off the LOS on a run or passing play. The perimeter corps is coached to drive off the LOS every time as if they were running a pass route. Fast driving arms and high knees relay to the defensive back that the receiver is releasing at full speed. Mastering the appearance of running full speed is a skill that all receivers must learn. The objective of the drive is to force the defender as deep as possible before initiating contact. The defender must be enticed to believe "pass" every time the receiver releases and drives off the wall. Consistency in the release and drive is the key to setting up the correct stalk position.

Breaking Down

The two elements in teaching the receiver to break down and prepare for contact are: first, identifying the defender's intention to abandon pass coverage and support the pitch, and second, "breaking down" between the defender and the ball carrier. *Breaking down* can be interpreted as gaining the final blocking position on the defender, then settling in to mirror his attack path to the ball.

The defender's intentions to abandon pass coverage are easily recognized when he directly attacks the LOS, or when he allows his cushion on the receiver to collapse. The blocker is coached to key the defender's hips. When the hips level out and square up, the blocker breaks down into a semi-crouched hitting position and prepares for collision.

The actual breakdown technique requires the blocker to lower and widen his base. The head is up, shoulders squared, and the feet are buzzing. The blocker maintains leverage by mirroring the defender's reaction. Patience is a key element that the blocker must develop in allowing the defender to "come in" to the block. An overaggressive or lunging block is easily side-stepped and avoided. The breakdown mirroring gives the defender only one route to the ball—through the block.

The Collision

Contact is made up through the defender's numbers. The blocker explodes up through the defender from his low buzzing base. The objective of collisioning is to stop the defender's momentum. Upon contact, the blocker divorces the defender, repositions and resets to pop again. The blocker continues to pop the defender until he "feels" the ball carrier. At this, the blocker cuts through the outside hip with a cross-body block. Once contact is made at the hip, the blocker pressures the defender's legs by crab-blocking on all fours. The blocker is taught to keep "alive" on all fours by keeping his head up field and his feet buzzing. Only as a last resort does the blocker roll through the defender's legs. Collisioning is a patient exploding and repositioning sequence that keeps the blocker between the defender and the ball carrier.

THE STALK BLOCK DRILL SEQUENCE

Three drills are incorporated to teach the stalk block to the perimeter corps.

Break Down Mirror Drill (Diagram 6-9)

Equipment: None
Objectives: 1. To develop the quick lateral shuffle required to mirror a defender's reaction.
2. Teach the initial explosion up through the defender.
Method: A receiver is paired up with a defensive counterpart five yards apart. On the command, both break down and buzz their feet. Positioned behind the blocker, the coach gives directional wave signals to the defender. The blocker mirrors this reaction, maintaining a good low hitting base. On the "up" signal, the defender commits up to the blocker. The blocker explodes up through the defender, divorces, and resets to conclude the drill.

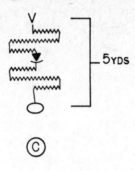

Diagram 6-9

Coaching Point:

The blocker is coached to focus on the defender's belt. The defender cannot fake with his hips.

The Stalk and Slip (S/S) Drill (Diagram 6-10)

Equipment: One tall cylinder dummy.

Objectives: 1. To teach the proper release and drive from the LOS.
2. To develop the breakdown and collision with a relatively non-mobile target.

Method: The dummy is held 15 yards upfield directly over the blocker. On cadence, the blocker drives upfield and gains an outside leverage on the bag. As the blocker approaches the bag, he breaks down and prepares for contact. The defender moves the bag into the blocker to simulate defensive reaction. The blocker explodes up through the bag, resets, and explodes again. After the third pop, the blocker cuts the outside hip with a cross-body block to tie up the defender's legs.

Coaching Points:

1. The defender holding the bag is encouraged to react slightly with the bag during the drill. This helps develop focusing and mirroring on a moving object.

2. For a variation, a defender is aligned over the receiver and instructed to delay his release. The receiver now develops evasive tactics off the LOS.

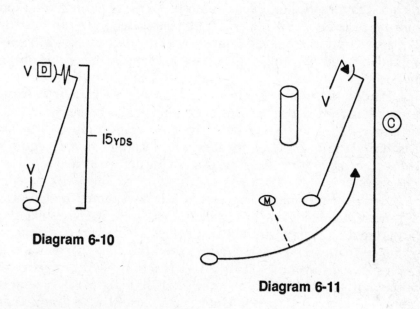

Diagram 6-10

Diagram 6-11

The Stalk Drill (Diagram 6-11)

Equipment: One tall dummy for a boundary and the sideline.

Objective: To teach the full stalk block in a controlled scrimmage situation.

Method: Align the blocker and defender inside the boundary lines in game situation positions. The manager (or QB) sets up in a pitch position. The BC is offset for timing purposes. On cadence, the receiver releases upfield on the stalk block. The pitch timing is similar to a live game situation. The defender reacts to the ball in normal assignment coverage. The objective of the drill is to break the long run up the sideline.

Coaching Point:

The defender is assigned by the coach to drop into coverage, then react up, squat in his area, or crash up for the pitch. The receiver must learn to recognize each move as he releases and drives to the block.

ALTERNATE BLOCKING SCHEMES FOR 32/33

There are four primary reasons for including alternate blocking schemes into the 30 series. First, defensive alignment may dictate a change. Second, weak defensive personnel can be attacked more effectively. Third, alternate blocking schemes can destroy defensive option schemes. Fourth, alternate schemes can be designed to create blocking angles that complement the option objectives.

The basic option schemes are effective, by design at least, versus standard defenses. However, alternate schemes create an offensive edge that makes defensive preparation more difficult. Disguising the base triple with alternate blocking schemes requires some internal adjustment, but is strategically necessary to offset defensive keys.

The first interior adjustment to the basic scheme is designed to aid the center's blocking assignment. Odd front defenses like the 5-2 present the center with a difficult block when the zero defender slants or shades into the playside. When the center anticipates a defensive slant into the playside gap (Diagram 6-12) or sees the nose guard shaded toward the playside (Diagram 6-13), his call is "zero." This releases the On Guard from his #1 man assignment and reassigns his block on the zero defender.

Now the On Guard's primary assignment is to assist the center's block. Diagram 6-12 illustrates the nose guard slanting into the playside gap. The On Guard blocks the noseguard's hip to stop lateral pursuit. The center reaches through the noseguard's playside breast and works for the upfield position. The On Guard's

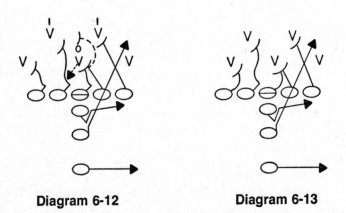

Diagram 6-12   Diagram 6-13

block merely sets the defender up until the center gains control. Should the zero defender slant away, the On Guard continues backside, looking to block the first pursuit toward the playside.

Diagram 6-13 illustrates the playside gap being threatened by the noseguard's shaded alignment. The "zero" call now gives the On Guard the primary responsibility for preventing the defender from penetrating the playside gap. The On Guard down blocks the zero defender to prevent lateral pursuit. The center supports the block by preventing penetration. The "zero" call by the center protects the center-guard gap.

The guard-tackle gap is threatened by shade alignments over the On Guard. The split 60 DT in Diagram 6-14 is in position to slant into the playside gap and make the On Guard's block difficult at best. Utilizing the "fold" block as an alternate to the base scheme seals the FB's dive crease. Diagram 6-14 illustrates the fold scheme. The On Tackle is assigned to collapse the #1 defender's outside slant with a down block. The On Guard steps laterally behind the OT on his way to sealing off the LBer's outside pursuit. The OG-OT gap must be reduced slightly to enable the fold scheme to develop quickly. The center is responsible to check any inside stunts from #2 before continuing toward the backside LB.

An alternate scheme to the fold block is diagramed in 6-15. An outside rub-double block by the On Tackle conforms to the standard triple option assignments but supports the On Guard's reach block on the #1 defender. The rub-double scheme assigns the On Tackle to collision the DT's outside hip long enough to allow the guard to reach toward the outside breast. The guard is responsible to gain the playside position by stepping through the

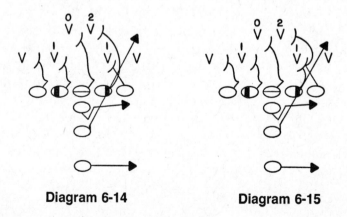

Diagram 6-14   **Diagram 6-15**

defender's outside foot. The tackle pops the DT, then rubs off onto his LB assignment. The rub-double is a quick-developing scheme. When used in conjunction with the fold block to seal the FB's dive crease, defensive option keys become obscured.

A creative weakside alternate scheme is designed to "sucker" the fourth defender. The "T-scheme" (Diagram 6-16) calls for an exchange of assignments between the On Tackle and the TE. Pulling the tackle on the slow arc influences the dive-read to step out on sweep pursuit. The ride/decide result becomes academic if the DT is well-drilled in reading and reacting to what he sees.

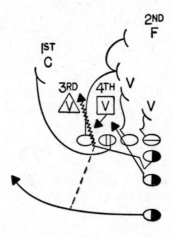

Diagram 6-16

The TE releases inside to seal off the first inside LBer's pursuit. If #1 is controlled by the On Guard, the TE continues downfield to stalk block the second defender. The inside release by the TE gives the defensive perimeter a false key for triple option development.

The pulling tackle is coached to break down and run through the first defender's numbers. The defensive back is recognized as having a quickness advantage over the OT. Therefore it is futile to ask the tackle to break down and mirror the defender's reaction. The tackle will be at a disadvantage trying to stalk block the defender. The tackle is coached to key the first defender's hips and pop the numbers.

A strongside corner roll (Diagram 6-17) forces the SE to set his stalk block too close to the LOS to be rationally effective. The "switch" scheme is designed to counter corner-roll pressure. The SE drives beyond the first defender's original position to intercept the rolling safety's outside release. The SE's stalk block is much more delayed and deeper downfield.

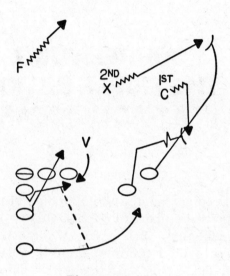

Diagram 6-17

The SLT must make his initial release upfield to give the secondary a "pass" read. The SLT is assigned to key the first defender. Once the roll begins, the SLT turns out and positions the corner's inside breast. The corner is kick blocked to the outside, which permits the pitchback to break underneath on his way to the SE's stalk block.

7

CORRELATING
THE TRIPLE OPTION
PLAY-ACTION PASS

A primary complementary component of the multiple option package is the play-action pass. Passing, like optioning, is dependent upon skill development, strategical inclusion, and an unprecedented commitment. The play-action pass is a valuable weapon that must be developed to complement the multiple option objectives. The triple option attacks the defense across a horizontal scale. The defensive front is stretched horizontally as the option play develops. The objective of the play-action pass is to option the defense on a vertical scale. The play-action pass offsets defensive overreaction to the run.

WHY INCORPORATE THE PLAY-ACTION PASS?

The play-action pass is not a luxury; it is a necessity. Option principles cannot work versus the nine- or ten-man fronts. Heavy or overloaded defensive fronts quickly outnumber the option at the perimeter. Releasing three receivers downfield loosens up the perimeter coverage. Secondary defenders are caught in a decision dilemma. Pitch-support dictates a commitment to the LOS while pass coverages dictate a minimum of three deep zones or men that must be covered. The perimeter defenders are caught in the vertical stretch. Play-action baits the secondary to commit to the pitch-support while being threatened by the deep pass.

A balanced run-and-pass attack gives the defense more to prepare for. The added preparation for defending a balanced option with a corresponding play-action holds defenses in more predictable alignments. Preparing for both the option and the pass prevents concentration on either phase of the offense.

The Twin-I incorporates the option play-action pass to balance out the run/pass ratio rather than as a surprise element. The objective for including play-action is to keep the defense off the LOS and aware of the possibility that the ball will be passed on any down. This relieves defensive pressures along the LOS and especially at the perimeter for stalk blocking.

A vital internal reason for balancing the play-action passing with the run is to take advantage of skilled receivers. The perimeter corps are drilled as blockers and receivers. The passing game is an incentive to motivate good blocking habits.

In the final analysis, the play-action pass is the balancing agent within the option package. The explosiveness of the running demands defensive commitment to the LOS. The natural companion to the triple option is a strategically designed play-action series.

WHEN TO USE THE PLAY-ACTION SERIES

Once confidence in the play-action pass has been accepted into the offensive scheme, almost any down or situation can be enhanced with play-action. The obvious exception, however, is the radical passing situation. The play-action fake wastes time and draws little respect in long yardage situations. But there are four situations where the play-action pass can be especially effective.

1. When defensive coverage or a single defender is obviously run-support oriented. The ball must be thrown when receivers are not respected in their downfield release routes. The option cannot develop when the defensive secondary crowds the LOS.

2. When defensive secondary personnel permit their coverage cushion on the receiver to collapse, they become susceptible to baiting routes (i.e., out and up, hook and go, or the pop pass). Play action is designed to promote a degree of honesty in secondary coverage.

3. When defensive alignment or rotation leaves vacancies in the coverage, inverting two deep zones can be attacked effectively by releasing three receivers deep. An alignment that does not cover the twin receivers is at an obvious disadvantage. Secondaries that

align or drop deep leave the short zones vulnerable to timed routes or backs out of the backfield.

4. The play-action pass is a premier candidate for opportunistic or gambling situations. These situations might include short yardage downs, the downs immediately after receiving a turnover or a big break, and even early downs coming out of the end zone.

Restricting series diversification and especially the inclusion of the play-action series has a domino effect on the development of the multiple option concept. If the multiple option concepts are to be effective, defenses must be optioned both horizontally along the LOS and vertically along the depth of the field.

DEVELOPING THE PLAY-ACTION BLOCKING SCHEME

Three fundamental principles are incorporated into the development of blocking schemes for the play-action series.

1. A simple format is essential to keep the additional learning to a minimum.
2. The play-action assignments need to conform as near as possible with the designed run-action counterparts.
3. The design and scheme must not give a quick defensive pass key. The play-action must be disguised through techniques and assignments.

Diagrams 7-1, 7-2, and 7-3 illustrate the basic 330 play-action pass protection assignments versus standard defensive fronts.

Off Guard: #1 defender, pivot technique.

Off Tackle: #1 defender, pivot technique.

Offside TE: As a general rule, the TE is released into the pass pattern. However, in the event that maximum protection is required, the term "Max" is added to the play selection. The TE is now responsible for the #3 defender through use of the pivot technique. An example of the play call requiring the TE to stay in is: Right 338 Z Takeoff "Max."

FB: Fake the dive into the LOS. Seal the OG-OT gap. If the OT steps down, seal the first defender to the outside.

TB: Open to the sideline, cross over on the third step and attack the #3 defender. Aggressive block as near to the LOS as possible.

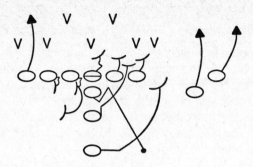

Diagram 7-1   Vs. 5–2

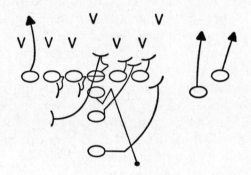

Diagram 7-2   Vs. 4–3

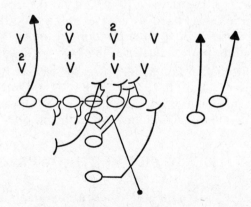

Diagram 7-3   Vs. 4–4

Coaching Point:

Each of the interior linemen has a man assignment. If the assignment is a LB, the blocker is responsible to pick up all stunts into the backside. If the LB does not stunt, and instead drops into pass coverage, the blocker is responsible to assist on the first defender to the offside. If the immediate defender is not a threat, the blocker swings to the back door. The purpose of the "back door" rule is to protect the QB from blindside hits.

The overall objective in the 330 design is to give the QB maximum protection behind the onside OT. The aggressive technique requires the onside blockers to rip up through their defender's outside breast and gain a pass protection position on the LOS. Once the defender's charge is stopped, the blocker divorces and resets for collision up in the LOS. The aggressive block dictates that the defender must be kept on the LOS.

The pivot technique is designed exclusively for backside protection in all play-action series. The objective for this technique requires that the initial block be set up on the LOS, which denies the defensive secondary an early pass key. There are three primary elements in the mechanics of the pivot technique.

1. The initial movement on cadence is a lateral playside step to shut off the inside gap. The inside gap is a direct route to the QB's setting position. The quick inside step protects against stunts or slants and gives the blocker a playside position advantage.

2. The blocker, immediately after closing the inside gap, pivots backward on the playside foot and breaks down in a hitting position. The backward pivot leaves only an outside route for the defensive rush. The proper position for the blocker after pivoting is almost perpendicular to the LOS.

3. After pivoting and breaking down, the blocker is coached to be patient and let the defender come to him. Once the defender commits to his rushing path, the blocker explodes up through the inside shoulder, forcing the rush to the outside.

BEATING DEFENSES WITH THE THROWBACK CONCEPT

Option defenses are having to commit two defenders to cover the pitch versus the spread option formations. Traditionally, run-support to the outside still left the defense with three-deep after rotating. The threat of the pitch developing on the corner has forced a change in most defensive schemes. The general rationale has become, "Stop the option first, then the pass." The pitch is most effectively stopped from the outside. Therefore, the final rotation leaves the defense with two deep defenders (Diagram 7-4). The throwback concept is designed specifically to attack the back door of the overload defensive rotation. The strongside triple option play action challenges the secondary rotation with play 338/339.

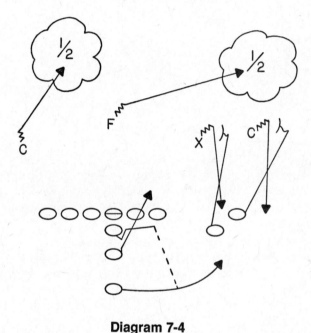

Diagram 7-4

The assignments for the interior line and backfield correspond to the standard 330 blocking scheme. The 338/339 pattern assignments and keys are diagramed in 7-5.

TE: The TE is assigned a post/takeoff route. The TE keys the free safety's reaction and runs the route to correspond with coverage. As the TE releases inside, he anticipates running the post route. His key is the safety's rotation. If the safety rotates over the top to the strong side, the TE immediately bends the post route inside the near corner and splits the seam difference with the deep safety. Should the safety squat or not react, the TE breaks the

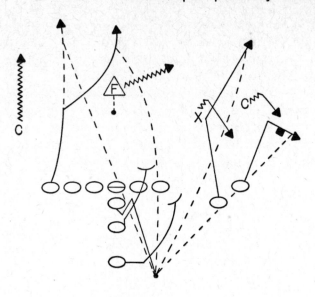

Diagram 7-5

takeoff route up the field. Both routes place the TE inside the corner and behind the safety. If the safety locks up on the TE, he then drives a deep clearing route, knowing that he is no longer the primary receiver.

SLT: The SLT is assigned to break a 10-step flag route. He also keys the free safety's rotation to determine his role in the play. The SLT drives to the second defender's inside breast. If the safety is rotating toward the playside, the SLT turns the flag deep to draw coverage. This widens the TE's post seam. Should the safety not rotate, the flag route is broken into the outside 1/2 zone and becomes the secondary target.

SE: The SE has the safety valve sideline route. This route requires the SE to drive ten steps upfield in a standard wide release. On the tenth step, the SE plants and comes back three yards toward the sideline. After squaring up to the QB, the SE hangs near the sideline, floating laterally to give the QB an easy target for completion or for overthrowing.

QB: After riding the FB into the LOS, the QB sets up in three steps behind the On Tackle. Three steps are generally 6 to 8 yards deep. On the set, the QB squares up to the LOS and keys the free safety's reaction. The QB's thought process is, "I will throw to the TE, unless the safety covers him." The secondary receiver is the flag route, followed by the SE on the sideline as a safety valve.

Play 338/339 is very effective versus quick-rotating secondaries. The TE in his throwback role is a constant reminder to the secondary to play the pass first. Both the post/takeoff and the flag routes quickly attack the defense deep. This vertical stretch is critical in controlling overloading or heavy rotation into the pitch.

The throwback concept is equally effective in supporting the weak side triple option. Play 334/335 is designed to capitalize on weakside rotation using the SE and SLT in the throwback routes. Like 338/339, the interior and backfield protection is the standard 330 scheme (Diagram 7-6).

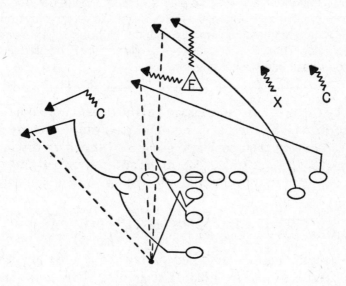

Diagram 7-6

SE: The SE is the primary target on the drag route. The SE takes a quick three-step release to allow the SLT to clear. The SE keys the free safety's rotation and splits that seam with the far corner. The SE must anticipate the reception under the safety and inside the far corner's rotation. Should the safety lock up on the drag route, the SE breaks back toward the LOS to open the SLT's deep slant route.

SLT: The SLT is assigned to release directly for the free safety's near hip and drive on a deep slant route upfield. The objective of the route is to drive the safety deep, opening up the SE drag. If the safety reacts up and does not respect the deep slant, the SLT continues deep, anticipating the long pass.

TE: The TE is assigned to release outside as if on the slow arc block. Once an outside position is gained on the first defender, the TE breaks to the sideline as the safety valve.

OB: The QB is instructed to ride the FB patiently and set at a three-step depth behind the On Tackle. The QB's thought process is: "I will throw to the SE unless the safety comes up." The secondary target is the deep slant route of the SLT, followed by the TE sideline as the safety valve.

Coaching Point:

A key component in selling the play-action fake to the defense is the QB's ride with the FB. Often, the QB is anxious to set up away from the LOS. A patient ride complements both the blocking scheme and the pass routes. The QB is coached to patiently ride the FB to his belt, then explode back into his set position.

The throwback concept is vital to the development of the base triple option. The threat of the deep pass causes defenses to be more cautious in their coverage designs. If the mere threat of the deep play-action pass will keep nine- and ten-men fronts off the LOS, its inclusion into the multiple option system is justified.

CAPITALIZING WITH THE POP PASS

The pop pass is designed to be a quick timing route to capitalize specifically on isolated secondary defenders that have been assigned pitch coverage. The pop route is a simple route that requires a combination of acting and skill. The basic pop routes for spread receivers are diagrammed in 7-7.

The route mechanics require the receiver to release directly at his covering defender. As the receiver reaches his fifth step on the release, he widens and lowers his base slightly, slowing down to simulate breaking down for the block. The objective for this technique is to draw the defender up on pitch-support or at least to stop his pass drop. Immediately on the fifth step the receiver fades away laterally and upfield from the defender. Once the receiver begins his fade, he is coached to check over the inside shoulder for the ball. His route is adjusted to fade upfield. This quick pass is a balancing weapon that keeps perimeter defenders off the LOS.

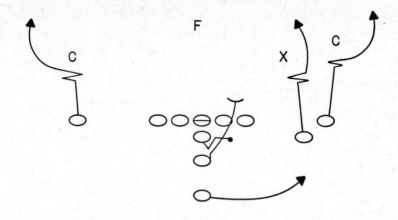

Diagram 7-7

The quick pass protection technique used for 332/333 is designed to keep the interior defender's hands down and to cut off lateral pursuit. The interior five are responsible for their base 330 man assignment. However, the quick pass protection technique dictates a uniform surge into the defender's playside hip. The blocker is coached to crab block through the defender's playside hip, collisioning immediately to neutralize slanting or stunts. The blocker's feet are kept buzzing to keep pressure on the defender.

The backfield assignments vary slightly from the basic 330 scheme.

FB: Dive hard and low through the LOS. Make a great handoff fake. Cut block the first defender to show.

TB: Explode on the pitch route. Draw pitch coverage with a good play-action fake.

QB: Ride the FB into the LOS. Immediately on the disconnect, bring the ball up through the throwing motion, releasing with a high arc to the designated pop route. The pass must be up on the QB's third step. This timing pass is quick and crisp but requires a lofting touch to allow the receiver to fade underneath. The target spot on the receiver is ideally over the outside shoulder away from coverage. The pass must lead the receiver away and upfield from the covering defender.

Play 332/333 is the most flexible quick pass in the multiple option arsenal. Its function is to isolate on specific defenders. This is

accomplished through formationing and identifying the defensive
option coverage. An example of defeating man coverage is illustrated in Diagram 7-8. Motion is used to create a one-on-one
situation for the SE. The corner can be attacked with the pop route
because pitch-support must, in part, come from the outside.

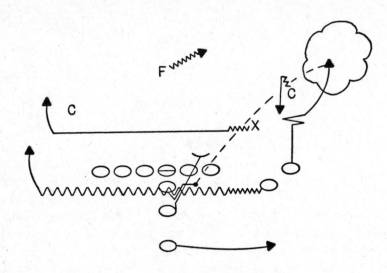

Diagram 7-8   Right Fly 332 Z Pop

Inverting pitch-support is countered with the Y pop route
(Diagram 7-9). The spread formation stretches the secondary horizontally, suggesting invert coverage to both sides of the formation.
The SLT releases toward the strong safety and acts out the stalk
block breakdown. Once the safety reacts to the option action, the
SLT breaks the pop route upfield, splitting the deep 1/3 seam
between the corner and the free safety.

Corner roll coverage into the TE side is susceptible to the X
pop (Diagram 7-10) route. The TE takes his lateral release to clear
the LOS and to widen the corner. The pop route breaks the TE
inside the corner's adjustment and up the seam in front of the
rotating safety. The QB modifies the pass to clear the LBer's and to
lead the TE away from the safety.

The pop pass, as a single component of the triple option play
action series, poses immediate problems for the secondary. Primarily, the nature of the route gives the appearance of run action. The
QB's quick release after the ride compounds the defensive reads.

The pop pass develops so fast from off a run fake that option defensive keys are stymied momentarily. This moment of indecision is the primary objective into the multiple option philosophy.

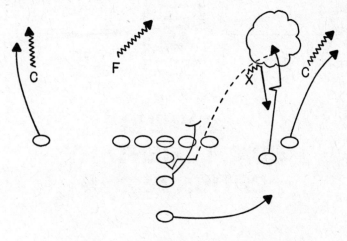

Diagram 7-9   Spread Right 332 Y Pop

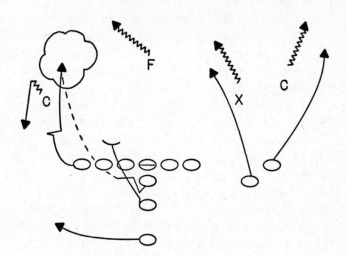

Diagram 7-10   Right 333 X Pop

8

WINNING
COMPLEMENTARY
OPTION SERIES

Superior personnel are required to achieve consistent success if the triple option is to be a single series offense. Defenses have become too complex in their strategies to neutralize the option's leverage points. For many years, option philosophy has been that of pure simplicity. Use of the triple option series with its standard counter option and play-action pass adaptations were all that were needed. However, defenses have now pushed the triple option series into becoming complex. This complexity is realized when a variety of "special" blocking and reading schemes are required to redefine original option vantage points. All option attacks surrender a portion of their effectiveness to the defense when they are forced to change fundamental blocking schemes and option reads. The option can adjust, and must if it is to survive. But with additional schemes and reads come more complex blocking patterns and more difficult QB interpretive situations.

The Twin-I multiple system incorporates four fundamental complementary option series to keep defenses honest in their design against the basic triple series. Each of these complementary series is designed to capitalize on structural or personnel weaknesses left by the defense in its game planning to stop the triple option. The basic philosophy behind this incorporation is twofold.

First, the team's optioning abilities must be utilized to a maximum. So much time is spent on teaching and training the option theory and thought process that the incorporation of a variety of option series is logical. Second, the installation of simple secondary series forces the defense to prepare for "one more thing." This multiple option philosophy makes game planning difficult for the defense. Should the triple be stopped first? Or should a balanced front be used to defend all possibilities from the multiple option arsenal? The defense must now consider priorities: "What do we defend first?"

Four basic option series constitute the alternate option game. All four are unique and each spins off the fundamentals taught for the progenitor of them all, the triple series. The four series are: the counter option, the counter trap option, the crazy option series, and the lead-out option, which is sometimes referred to as the "speed" option.

Of the four complementary series, three are of misdirection descent. Their value is obvious against the defense that quick-reads and overpursues the triple option. The lead-out series is a quick-developing double option, but possesses misdirection potential as will be explained later in this chapter.

The primary objective of including these specific complementary series is to force the defense to stay home and "watch the back door." Defenses thrive on pursuit and outnumbering the option at the perimeter. The triple option slows down defensive pursuit, but misdirection option series *stop* it.

CONTROLLING DEFENSES WITH COUNTER OPTION— THE 20 SERIES

The counter option is the simplest method of incorporating a misdirection key for defenses. The 20 series is broken down into two separate components, the counter dive and the counter option. There are five basic advantages that are gained from the 20 series.

1. The counter series capitalizes quickly to the weak side of the formation versus defenses that slant their front into the formation side or wide side of the field.

2. The counter action creates a quick-read problem for interior defenders who key the QB for directional tendencies.

3. The FB does not counter step. Therefore, the counter dive hits the LOS much faster than from other option alignments. This quick-hitting counter takes immediate advantage of overpursuing LBers (Diagram 8-1).

4. The QB/FB mesh for the 20 series is smooth and prompt. This facilitates the rapid development of the counter option at the perimeter. The QB disconnects from the FB farther removed from the option point, giving him more read time and a direct downhill angle from which to create the option advantage. The 20 series double option attacks the perimeter much faster than from a split backfield.

5. The quick counter mesh with the FB is highly conducive to play-action pass sequels. Counter series play-action freezes interior LBers longer than the pure triple play action.

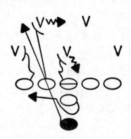

Diagram 8-1

Play 24/25—the Counter Dive

The counter dive gets the ball to the FB very quickly and very close to the LOS. This exchange is hidden from interior LBers and perimeter defenders (i.e., defensive ends and stacked LBers). The FB's alignment is directly behind the QB, which allows him to take a mesh step to the point of attack without being detected. The double option fake down the LOS after the mesh draws the perimeter defenders outside, opening up the dive crease. Diagrams 8-2 and 8-3 illustrate this principle. The base assignments for 24 and 25 are as diagramed in 8-4 and 8-5.

Center: Over, backside LB.

On Guard: #1 outside breast. (Note—this block is the drive block. The QB/FB mesh is directly behind the On Guard. His block must be upfield to permit the QB his downhill attack angle.)

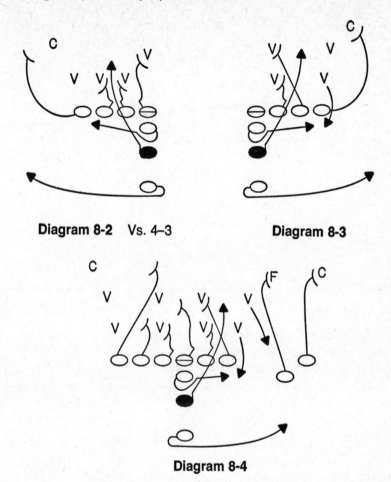

Diagram 8-2   Vs. 4–3   **Diagram 8-3**

Diagram 8-4

On Tackle:	#2 ballside-breast. (The term "ballside breast" is used to denote the possible position of the #2 defender. Diagram 8-2 places #2 aligned head up, therefore the inside breast is the target point. Diagram 8-3 places #2 at an inside stacked LB. Down blocking attacks the LBer's outside breast.)
Off Guard:	#1 inside breast.
Off Tackle:	#2 inside breast. When the defender's feet are stopped, release downfield to set up cutback blocks.
TE-On:	Outside release for first defender. (This wide release draws pitch-support defenders outside.) Stalk block widest defender.
-Off:	Inside release for middle safety. Flatten off release to get a lead position on the defender.

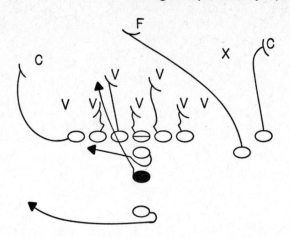

Diagram 8-5

Coaching Point:

Downfield clips must often occur when a backside blocker trails the defender, then blocks him from behind. The flat release puts the blocker between the defender and the ball.

SE-On: Drive off the first defender and stalk block.

  -Off: Flat release across to cut off first defender.

SLT-On: Inside stalk on second defender.

   -Off: Inside flat release on second defender.

FB: Landmark the outside hip of the On Guard. Take the short playside step. Mesh with the QB on second step. Cover the ball and veer to daylight off the guard's block.

Coaching Point:

The young FB will tend to raise up on the first step. This elevates the QB's table top mesh and makes the FB visible for the LBers to key. The FB is coached to stay low from the stance to the mesh and on through the LOS.

TB: Counter step and sprint the highway to the sideline. Fake the pitch route.

QB: Counter step and mesh with the FB. Ride into LOS before giving the ball. After mesh, sprint downhill at the OP and fake the pitch or the keep.

Coaching Point:

Teaching the QB to fake the keep upfield after the mesh will draw the secondary into the pitch-support many times, taking them out of the dive crease. This occurs primarily because the QB keep and the pitch are a legitimate threat.

Play 28/29—The Counter Option

The 20 series counter option is a double option. This simply means there will be a predetermined disconnect from the FB, and only the keep/pitch phase of the option will be executed. Many times the question is asked, "Why isn't the triple read executed from the counter?" The I formation appears to facilitate a possible triple read from counter action. However, the triple option's success primarily stems from the fact that the QB can focus on the dive-read from the snap on. Having the QB counter step breaks the visual contact for the give/disconnect decision. This would result in the QB guessing with the dive-read for the give or disconnect.

The counter option attacks the perimeter immediately. There is no hesitation step for the QB on his counter step and mesh with the FB. The QB disconnects from the FB and attacks the OP directly. With the predetermined disconnect from the FB, the FB can become an effective blocker, sealing off any pursuit from the inside. Diagram 8-6 illustrates the assignments for 28/29 versus a 40 defense, and Diagram 8-7 outlines the counter option versus the 5–2 odd front.

Center: Over backside LB through the playside gap.
On Guard: #1 outside breast.
On Tackle: #2 outside breast, man over.

Coaching Point:

The tackle's block must be on the LOS against a man-over alignment. The FB is assigned to pick up any stacked LBer.

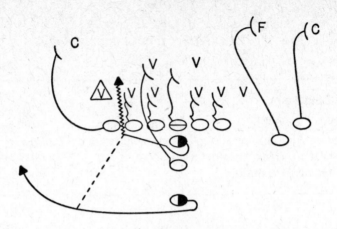

Diagram 8-6

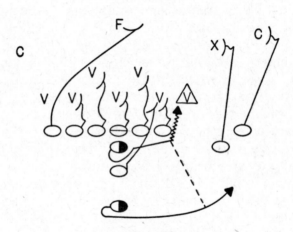

Diagram 8-7

Off Guard:	#1 inside breast through the playside gap.
Off Tackle:	#2 inside breast.
TE:	Onside: Outside release to stalk block widest defender. Offside: Inside release flat across the field.
SE:	Onside: Stalk first defender. Offside: Flat across field to safety.
FB:	Counter dive fake into LOS. Remain low to draw a tackle. Seal block first LB inside of the crease.
TB:	Counter step, sprint pitch route, expect a quick pitch.
QB:	Counter mesh with FB. Disconnect and attack the third defender. Thought process: "I will keep unless I read pitch."

Coaching Point:

The QB must be cautioned not to disconnect too soon. This will put the option path too deep in the backfield. The FB must be ridden into the LOS to create the valid fake and to adjust the downhill angle toward the OP.

Even though 28/29 is designed to attack the weak side of the formation, the series can be successfully executed to the twin side. The object of option football is to ultimately get the ball on the perimeter with the pitch. Incorporating the "G" scheme into the counter option toward the twin side frees up perimeter receivers to seal down to the inside and prevent quick pursuit by inside LBers (Diagram 8-8).

Three adjustments to 28/29 are incorpoated to capitalize with the "G" scheme. First, the SLT seal blocks inside. Second, the On Guard is pulled to block the pitch-support defender. And third, the FB seals for the pulling guard.

The seal block to the inside serves two purposes. First, the quick release must encourage the second defender to fade to the inside, rather than flatten out into a pitch-support position. Second, the seal block must occur inside the option point. The QB's keep path should be behind the seal block if the defensive read indicates keep.

The On Guard's arc pull must not interfere with the third defender at the option point. The guard is coached to get depth on

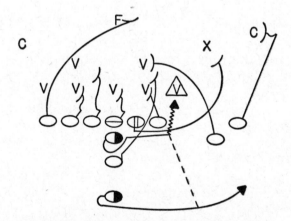

Diagram 8-8   "G" Scheme Vs. 52 Stack

his third lateral step. This depth divorces him from the option point and places him outside to gain a blocking angle on the pitch-support defender (see Diagram 8-9).

The third technique adjustment is that of the FB filling for the pulling guard. The FB must determine pre-snap who he will wham. If the OG is covered, the choice is automatic. Should the OG be uncovered, the FB is responsible for the first color over and to the backside of the OG alignment. Diagram 8-8 illustrates a change in assignment between the OT and the FB. Stacks over the OG box must be treated as a possible stunting alignment. Therefore, the OT will seal the most dangerous defender (the defensive tackle), and the FB will slip off to cut off the stacked LBer.

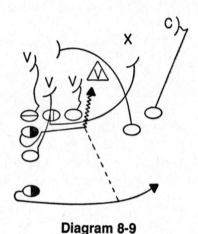

Diagram 8-9

COACHING THE COUNTER TRAP OPTION—50 SERIES

There are four primary reasons for installing the counter trap option into the Twin-I multiple option package.

1. The 50 series is built around a quick-hitting FB trap over the center. Preparing for the trap and the option requires two distinct theories and techniques. The defense must spend time to prepare for both.
2. This quick trap is complemented by the trap option. The trap option utilizes the fundamental optioning skills that are rehearsed daily.

3. The counter trap is designed to capitalize on defenses that align outside to overplay the option. Diagram 8-10 illustrates the counter trap versus the 6–2 defense. The defense, by alignment, is considered very strong versus the triple, but vulnerable to the quick trap.

4. Standard option blocking assignments tend to become monotonous for the linemen. Most schemes are of the man-over concept for the #1, #2 assignment. Trapping gives the lineman a chance to create angles to control larger defenders and to simply get the "good block." Trapping breeds enthusiasm for the interior personnel and creates headaches for the defender who is playing option assignment football.

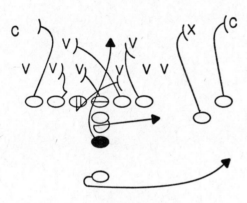

Diagram 8-10

Play 50/51—The Counter Trap

The counter trap is very effective for a variety of reasons. First, the diving FB is virtually undetectable by interior defenders. Second, the QB's counter pivot gives the defense a false key. Defenses who key the QB to determine the option's direction are easily misled. The key reason for installing the trap to the multiple option package is to force inside defenders to stay home expecting the trap. Preparing for traps requires tremendous defensive time and drilling. Defensive game planning must now take away time from option defense to concentrate on a foreign element, the trap. When the defense respects the trap potential possessed by the offense, its own game plan slows down pursuit into the perimeter.

The counter trap rules are diagramed versus several standard defensive fronts (Diagrams 8-11, 8-12, and 8-13). Of all trapping schemes, the FB counter trap requires the least time to perfect.

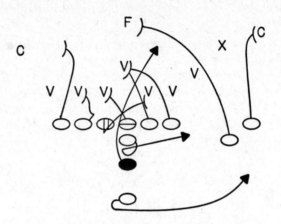

Diagram 8-11   Vs. 4–3

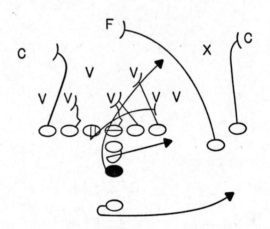

Diagram 8-12   Vs. 5–2

Center:	Over if covered, then fill for trapping guard.
On Guard:	First LB inside. Rub-double if center is covered.
On Tackle:	First LB to the inside. Drive LB through the POA.
Off Guard:	Trap inside-out on first down lineman on the LOS at or outside the POA.
Off Tackle:	#2 inside breast.
TE:	Inside release for widest defender.
Slot:	Inside release for deep safety.

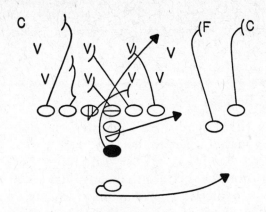

Diagram 8-13   Vs. 4–4

SE: Drive off and stalk the widest defender. (Note: Driving off
           the SE on deep outside routes sets up deep passes off the
           play-action. The takeoff is available for the corner who
           doesn't respect the SE driving deep on the inside dive.)

FB: Landmark the middle seam of the center's pants. Receive
           the mesh on the second step. Jump into the trapping
           guard's upfield hip pocket and cut behind the On Tackle's
           block.

TB: Counter step and carry out the pitch route fake.

QB: Open in the direction of the POA. Reverse pivot meshing
           with the FB. Ride the FB into the LOS completing a 360°
           pivot. Continue downhill faking the double option at the
           perimeter.

Coaching Point:

The QB's reverse pivot is a quick spin on the playside foot. The QB
opens with a short onside step, then spins back around to mesh with
the FB. The ball is kept in the "third hand" until the QB faces the FB.
The QB extends the ball into the FBs pouch with both hands and rides
until his spin action draws his hands out. The QB is cautioned not to lay
the ball out in one hand on the exchange. The FB will knock the ball out
with his inside elbow unless the ball is firmly placed inside the pouch.

The counter trap presents a difficult problem for defensive
teams that are schooled in the assignment tradition. Assignments

are confused with regard to the FB's dive path and the trap blocking. The primary objective of the 50/51 is to force the defense to be
conscious of the FB. This consciousness keeps interior defenders
from overpursuing at the perimeter.

Play 58/59—The Trap Option

Defenses who defend the FB first in their triple option game
planning are generally alert to the counter trap. When the diving
FB has attracted the interior LBer's attention, the counter trap
option stands a good chance of succeeding. Play 58/59 incorporates
crack blocking schemes at the perimeter to seal inside pursuit. The
pulling backside guard gives inside LBers a false trapping key. The
two combined complement the counter trap double option at the
perimeter.

All option series must create their own advantages over the
defense. The QB's reverse pivot does exactly that. After the QB
disconnects from the FB and completes the counter spin, he is deep
inside the LOS facing downhill toward the option point. This
position gives the QB a quick look at the option point for the
crashing defensive end, or for the quick off-tackle crease left from
defenders who isolated on the diving FB.

The trap option rules are designed to simulate the quick trap
action. The similarity is intended to freeze inside defenders with
false keys. Diagrams 8-14 and 8-15 depict the trap option assignments.

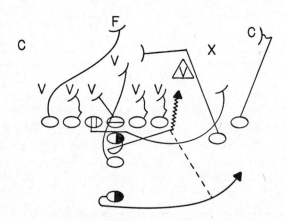

Diagram 8-14   Vs. 4–3

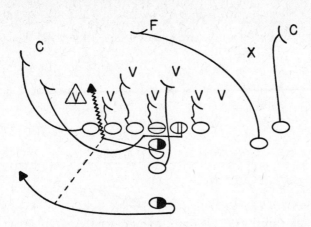

Diagram 8-15   Vs. 5–2

Center:	Over, fill for pulling guard.
On Guard:	#1 outside breast through the playside gap.
On Tackle:	#2 outside breast through the playside gap.
Off Guard:	Arc block on pitch responsible defender.

Coaching Point:

The Off Guard must deepen into the backfield on his third step. This allows the arc block to gain a relative position versus the outside defender. Also, the guard's deepening permits the QB to clearly visualize the option point.

Off Tackle: #2 inside breast.

Coaching Point:

The tackle's block is critical throughout the play. The trap option is slower in developing because of the counter step. A quick penetrating defensive tackle could chase the QB from behind.

TE:	Offside—Inside release to stalk the deep safety.
	Onside—Arc on widest defender.
Slot:	Offside—Flat release to keep safety.
	Onside—Crack inside on first pursuit.

SE: Deep outside release and stalk block first defender.

FB: Dive through the center's hip. Wham block the first LB inside-out.

TB: Counter step and sprint the pitch route.

QB: Reverse pivot mesh with the FB. Disconnect and square shoulders to the OP. Attack the third defender. Thought process is, "I will keep unless I read pitch."

Coaching Point:

The QB will be most effective if a patient attitude is exercised through the FB mesh and ride. If the ride is hurried, the QB will lose his balance in reestablishing the correct downhill path. The QB must permit the pulling guard to clear for the arc block.

Executing 58/59 into the weak side can be just as effective as into the twin set. However, one adjustment to the formation creates a tremendous offensive advantage. Diagram 8-16 illustrates the weakside side trap option from the spread formation. The TE is now responsible to crack inside on the primary pitch-support defender. The pulling guard must be ready to arc on the widest defender or kick out should cloud coverage come to force the pitch.

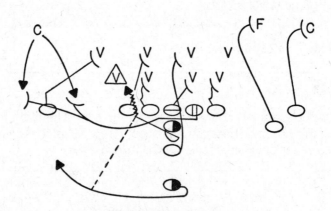

Diagram 8-16   Vs. 4–4

PRESSURING DEFENSES WITH THE CRAZY OPTION—
40 SERIES

The crazy option series is designed to attack into the weak side of the formation. The logic behind this selection of POA is to take advantage of the overshifted defense. This series can only be operable from the slot formation or by using the Zip motion to place Y into the slot position.

The 40 series is the most unique of the complementary option series. This series combines the TB counter trap and the trap option (with Y as the pitchback) into a very clever misdirection package. The primary objective for including the 40 series into the multiple option game plan is to take advantage of two situations. First, the defense who keys QB/FB direction as a primary pursuit key is seduced into a false read. Both the QB and the FB open away from the intended POA. Secondly, the trap phase of the crazy option series is designed to capitalize directly at alignments outside 2/3 point which are trappable. Many defensive alignments leave themselves vulnerable to the trap at the perimeters. The TB counter trap and the crazy option are logical partners to the triple and the 50 series counter trap option. The versatility of the 40 series is refreshing to option game planning.

Play 42/43—The Crazy Trap (The TB Counter Trap)

The TB trap offers an option attack two distinct advantages. First, this weakside attack neutralizes the slanting front. Odd front defenses especially have a tendency to slant into the strength of the formation or toward FB direction. The countering TB quickly challenges the overeager LBer who moves to the FB key. Second, the 40 series in general is a short-side series which is designed to counter defenses that defend the wide side of the field by radically overshifting and using the sideline for their twelfth man. The Twin formation tends to draw defensive attention to the strength of the formation. This weakside quick trap is safe to execute anywhere on the field. Either coming out or going in, the simplicity of the 40 series mechanics reduces incident or error.

The rules for 42/43 are illustrated in Diagrams 8-17 and 8-18. The assignments are similar to the 50 series. This similarity in trapping terms and rules reduces the learning time.

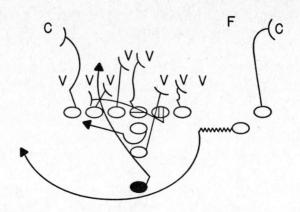

Diagram 8-17   Vs. Split 60

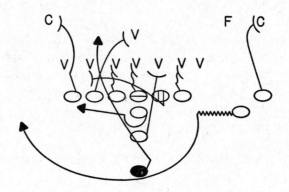

Diagram 8-18   Vs. Goalline 7–1

Center:	Over, backside LBer.
On Guard:	#1 outside breast.
On Tackle:	#2 outside breast.
Off Guard:	Trap inside-out on first defender on the LOS on or outside the POA.
Off Tackle:	#2 inside breast.
TE:	Inside release on most dangerous defender upfield. Note: This is generally the corner or a stacked LB.
SE:	Drive off and stalk block first defender.
Slot:	Drop step and sprint to gain a 4 × 4-yard pitch relation with the QB.
FB:	Dive fake away from POA. Wham block the defender over the pulling guard.

TB: Step away, cross over, and key the trapping guard's inside hip. Mesh with the QB on the third step. Look for TE's block downfield.

QB: Open the FB, quick-fake the handoff. (Note: this fake is a short ride on the FB's inside hip.) Counter step and mesh with the diving TB. Ride the TB into the LOS before giving the ball. Continue downhill faking the pitch route with trailing slot.

Play 48/49—The Crazy Option

The crazy option is a very unique method of executing the double option from the Twin-I formation. At first appearance, 48/49 could be classified as a trick or special situation play. However, its effectiveness as part of the multiple option game plan is unparalleled. When both I backs are committed into the LOS from trapping action, standard defensive option assignments are confused. The QB counter is in fact very delayed after faking to the FB and short-riding the TB. This delay forces the perimeter defenders to react to the trap. The slot's pitch route is obscured from the defenders at the POA. The QB's counter action allows the slot to gain the proper pitch relation.

The crazy option is diagramed in 8-19 versus the 53 defense and in 8-20 versus the split 60 front.

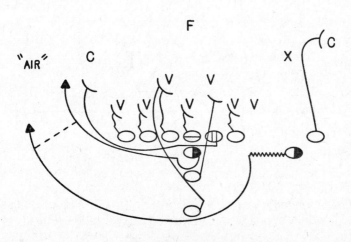

Diagram 8-19

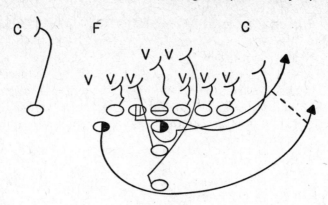

Diagram 8-20

Center: Over backside LB.

On Guard: #1 outside breast.

On Tackle: #2 outside breast.

Off Guard: Arc pull on pitch responsible defender.

Off Tackle: #2 inside breast.

TE: #3 outside breast. The TE must work upfield preventing the defender from stringing out the option.

SE: Drive off and stalk first defender.

Slot: Quickly establish a 4 × 4-yard pitch relationship with the QB. Get proper depth by sprinting through the TB's original position.

FB: Fake dive away from POA. Wham block defender over the pulling guard.

TB: Short mesh with the QB. Penetrate the OG and OT gap. Seal off first LBer inside out.

QB: Counter step with a fake jab to FB. Reverse pivot and short ride with the TB. The TB ride must continue to the QB's lead step. Disconnect and attack the perimeter. The thought process is, "I will keep unless I read pitch."

Coaching Point:

After disconnecting from the TB, the QB attacks the outside hip of the TE's block. All defenders have been accounted for in the blocking design; therefore, the QB attacks the perimeter and options "air," or the first defender to show outside the TE. The QB is taught to float in behind the pulling guard's arc to create an upfield angle. The arc block is designed to support the pitch. The QB must first challenge the keep.

INSTRUCTING THE LEAD-OUT OPTION—TEEN SERIES

Play 18/19 is the basic option pattern in the teen series. This double option is perhaps the most basic within the option family tree. The strength of this series is its quick attack on the perimeter. This directness forces the defense to commit its option assignments immediately.

As stated earlier, the prime objective of optioning is to get the ball on the corner. The teen series is bilateral. This forces the defense to balance its option assignments. When the defense commits to a balanced front, perimeter crack angles are set for the offensive receivers. These crack angles from the perimeter play a key role in the load options success. This angle literally prevents the pitch-responsible defender from attacking the LOS. The spread formation also puts the TE out into a crack alignment. This alignment not only stretches the secondary's area of coverage, but gives the TE a vantage point from which to select the defender responsible to cover the pitch. Crack angles are essential in setting up the teen series blocking scheme.

The blocking assignments will be broken up in two parts for discussion purposes. The first treats the basic interior line scheme; the second treats the perimeter schemes, which revolve around defensive alignment. Diagrams 8-21 and 8-22 illustrate the completed 18/19 option assignments.

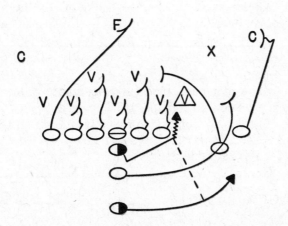

Diagram 8-21   Vs. 5–2

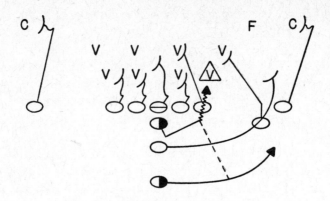

Diagram 8-22   Vs. 4–4

Center: Over, backside LB.
On Guard: #1 outside breast through the playside gap.
On Tackle: #2 outside breast.
Off Guard: #1 inside breast through the playside gap.
Off Tackle: #2 inside breast.

The 1–2 blocking scheme for the interior personnel keeps this series simple to install and isolates the defender to be optioned. The twin side assignments must be discussed.

SE: Stalk block first defender. Keep an outside angle to drive him deep.
Slot: Onside—crack on the first LBer off the LOS from the outside-in.

Coaching Point:

The inside LBers are potentially the most dangerous to the lead series. Their ability to slide outside and upfield is unchecked by a dive back. The slot can functionally outposition this threat. Stacked LBers as pictured in 8-22 and inside defenders as noted in 8-21 are just two examples of the slot's inside assignment.

Slot: Offside—flat release across the field to deep safety.

The TE rules are the most demanding to teach:

TE: Onside from a normal alignment—the TE is governed by the "3–2" rule. If there are three defenders aligned over or to the outside (Diagram 8-23), he must take an outside release and stalk block the widest defender. This is usually the corner. Should there be two defenders (Diagram 8-24) aligned over or to the outside, the TE combo blocks down on the first LBer.

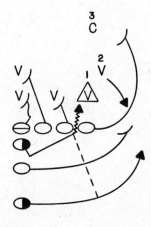
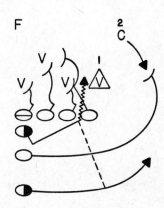

Diagram 8-23   "3–2" Rule Vs. 5–3   **Diagram 8-24**   "3–2" Rule Vs. 5–2

TE: Onside from the spread formation—the TE must be schooled from scouting reports as to which defender is responsible for the pitch into the weak side. As a general rule, the eight-man front such as the 44, 60, or 53 (Diagram 8-25) fronts, pitch-support comes from the inside-out. This is usually an outside LB or defensive end. A seven-man front generally supports the pitch from an outside-in. The TE rule is: crack first outside LB versus three-deep; drive off and stalk block first defender against four-deep.

TE: Offside—release inside to seal off the deep safety.

The Teen series backfield rules are designed to get on the perimeter immediately. The double option draws a rapid commitment from the defense as to their option coverage assignments.

FB: Arc block on the pitch-responsible defender.

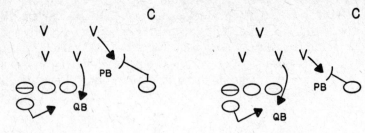

Diagram 8-25a   Vs. 4–4   **Diagram 8-25b**   Vs. 60

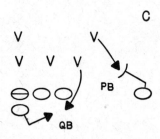

Diagram 8-25c   Vs. 53

Coaching Point:

The FB must be coached to run his arc route wide of the option point. Should the FB flatten out before the option point, he will interfere with the QB's read and be late in getting into the perimeter blocking scheme. Diagram 8-26 illustrates an incorrect route taken by the FB. The FB is crowding the QB's downhill angle. Diagram 8-27 demonstrates the proper arc path that is taught to put the FB in the most advantageous blocking position. As the FB clears the OT, he squares his hips upfield and focuses on the anticipated pitch-support defender. The FB is coached to attack the outside hip of the defender across the LOS.

TB: Sprint the pitch route. Expect a very quick pitch.
QB: On the snap, drop step with the playside foot to clear the LOS. The first step should also be pointed downhill. The second step should be directly at the inside hip of the defender at the OP. Diagram 8-28 illustrates the footwork. The QB immediately attacks the inside hip of the end defender, exercising the standard thought process, "I will keep unless I read pitch."

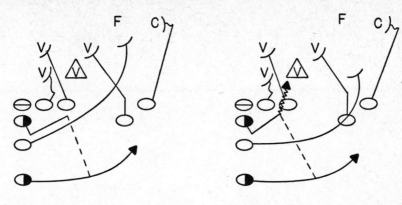

Diagram 8-26 Incorrect FB Arc   **Diagram 8-27** Correct FB Arc

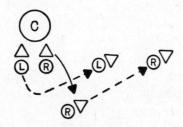

Diagram 8-28

There are three adjustments to the teen series which are designed to neutralize specific defensive schemes. The first is the "load" scheme (Diagram 8-29). The load scheme is incorporated to seal off the crashing end and get the QB into the perimeter to option the pitch-support defender. Many defensive coaches will crash the end to force the pitch. Their philosophy is sound in that once the ball is pitched, the pursuit will overpower the perimeter blocking schemes to stop the option.

The load scheme (18/19 load) assigns the FB to cut the outside hip of the crashing end. The QB sets up this block by stepping down the LOS in a normal attacking relation to draw the end in. On the second step off the ball, the QB veers behind the FB's cut block and turns upfield to challenge the pitch-support defender.

The crashing DE creates serious problems for the option attack. An early commitment to the pitch gives the defense an edge. The second adjustment to the teen series is also designed to get the DE's attention. The zip-load scheme assigns the slot to seal the DE to the inside (Diagram 8-30).

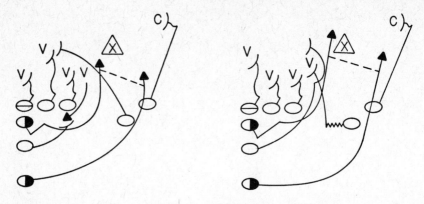

Diagram 8-29   "Load" Scheme   **Diagram 8-30**   "Zip-Load" Scheme

The timing between the slot and the QB must be perfected to set the block on the DE from short motion. The FB is assigned to "clean up" the outside hip of the DE should the zip-load not settle. If the slot has settled onto the block, the FB rubs off, looking for the first inside pursuit. The QB drops into a quick attack on the perimeter by getting immediate depth to clear the load block. The QB's hips must get square upfield once the block is cleared. This load scheme keeps defensive ends alert to more than just their option assignment.

The third adjustment is the simple addition of the backfield counter action (Diagram 8-31). Should the defense be coached to fly immediately on any backfield key, the counter holds the defenders in place long enough to allow the offensive blocking

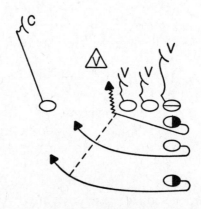

Diagram 8-31

scheme to develop. The incorporation of the counter action does require the three inside blockers (guards and center) to close off the center-guard gaps. The QB's counter action does not permit him to get as much distance from the LOS. A penetrating defender can create a fumble or push the option too deep into the backfield to permit the proper developmental process.

9

SERIES SPECIALTIES: THE WINNING EDGE

The Twin-I multiple option is designed to attack defenses in a variety of methods. The basic triple option, the complementary option series, the play-action pass, and as will be discussed in following chapters, the wide open passing game, all serve strategic purposes in the overall design of the multiple option package. Each in its own way contributes to the effectiveness of the option philosophy. However, it is the special plays that spin off these fundamental series that multiply the "big play" dimensions.

These special plays, or series specialties, likewise serve a unique role in the multiple option scheme. The specialty plays are designed to give an assignment-conditioned defense an unusual twist from the ordinary developing sequence. The objective of the specialty plays is to combine a simulated option format with the big play concept. The series specialties are not regarded as trick plays, but rather as the polishing dimension in the multiple option concept.

BEATING DEFENSES WITH THE OPTION PASS

The term option pass generally gives reference to the traditional halfback pass commonly used. The option pass in the Twin-I package is in fact a two-dimensional triple option. On the snap, the QB's options are to pass the ball deep or execute the trap series double option. Play 558/559 is designed to option the defense vertically and horizontally at the same time.

The option pass is designed exclusively to attack the strong side of the formation. The primary objective is to get the ball to the SE on the takeoff route followed by the double option at the perimeter. The strongside corner is isolated as the primary pass/ option key. The third defender remains the secondary keep/pitch read. The assignments for 558/559 are illustrated in Diagrams 9-1 and 9-2.

An aggressive quick pass blocking technique is used along the LOS. The blockers are coached to anticipate the pass, but to maintain an aggressive playside position on their assigned defender to prevent lateral pursuit. The TE is included in this option pass scheme for maximum protection to the backside. The SLT is instructed to assist in the overall blocking scheme primarily to give the secondary a run key and to seal off LBer pursuit should the option read predicate the double option. The composite blocking assignments are designed to give the defense a run key in supporting the first option, the deep pass.

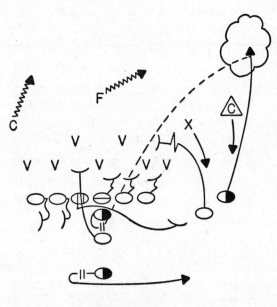

Diagram 9-1

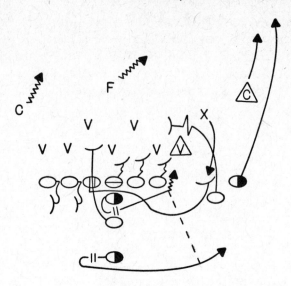

Diagram 9-2

Center: Over, or fill for the pulling offside guard.
On Guard: #1 outside breast, aggressive technique.
On Tackle: #2 outside breast, aggressive technique.
Off Tackle: #2 inside breast, pivot technique.
TE: #3 inside breast, pivot technique.

Coaching Point:

The aggressive technique is a low driving block through the playside hip that is designed to keep the defender's hands low to clear the throwing lane. This technique also requires immediate contact into the LOS to clear the QB's attack angle toward the option point.

Off Guard: Arc block to the playside. Turn upfield after gaining a
               blocking position on the pitch-support defender.

Coaching Point:

The Off Guard is coached to take his first two steps laterally down the LOS. This permits the QB to operate without interference in the backfield. Immediately after clearing the QB, the OG arcs back three to four yards to clear the option point and gain an outside position on the pitch-support defender. The OG need not worry about being downfield on the pass if his arc is deep enough into the backfield. Should the read be "pass," the OG will be in the arc path, but not across the LOS.

SLT: Crack block the first LBer off the LOS from the outside-in. Release immediately to the inside and begin breaking down to show run. Let the LB come to the crack block. This avoids the infraction of blocking downfield during a pass.

SE: Take the wide release off the LOS and drive deep on the takeoff route. Key the first defender for the pass key. If this defender has reduced his cushion or has committed up to the LOS, look immediately over the inside shoulder for the pass. Always check the pass on the fifth step off the LOS (Diagram 9-1). Continue to streak upfield if the defender remains in pass coverage. Drive him as deep as possible away from the double option (Diagram 9-2).

FB: Fake the trap hand off into the LOS. Set up and seal the first LBer from the inside-out. If a stunt does not develop, assist the center's block on the LOS.

TB: Take two steps to the offside before countering and sprinting the pitch route. A quick single-step counter will place the pitch much too wide for the QB in the event of an option read. Belly slightly away from the LOS to be in position to follow the OG's arc block at the perimeter.

QB: Pivot on the onside foot and open inside to the FB dive. Make a quick jab fake into the FB's pouch with the ball while planting the first step away from the LOS. After the fake to the FB, pivot on the first step toward the option point until the second step is planted. (The QB is now square to the option point and the second step has drawn him about three yards off the LOS.) Bring the ball up into a set position while locating the first defender to the strong side. Immediately set and buzz the feet while reading pass or option. The QB's thought process is, "I will pass the ball unless the corner deepens." If the corner deepens on coverage, the QB quickly attacks downhill on the double option (Diagram 9-3).

Coaching Point:

The QB has two counts after setting up to pass the football. Any further delay jeopardizes the interior blocking scheme. If the pass is not up in two counts, the trap option is executed. The pass key is an immediate read. If the quick pass is covered, it must be forgotten. It is futile to force a pass of this nature. The double option stands a very good chance of succeeding if the secondary has dropped to cover the pass.

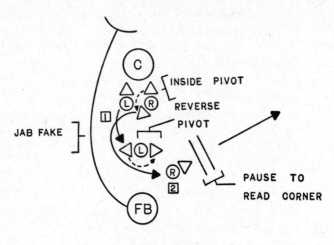

Diagram 9-3

CAPITALIZING WITH THE PLAY-ACTION QUICK PASS

The short pass off the lead option series gives this offense a quick-punch dimension. The quick pass, in general, is highly adaptable to the twin alignment's spread concept. There are five reasons why the teen series and the spread formation are selected for the play-action quick pass in the multiple option system.

1. The teen series is bilateral. The base lead-out option is unrestricted to either side of the formation. Therefore, the play action fake is very convincing to the defense.

2. The teen series requires no faking or meshing in the backfield. The QB controls the football without interference.

3. The QB does not set to pass. His simulated movement toward the option point persuades defensive reaction. As long as the QB has the ball and is moving down the LOS, the defense must respect the option threat.

4. The spread formation stretches the secondary to its maximum spread. Quick pass routes have a very high completion rate percentage.

5. The Twin alignment creates a natural clearing surge off the LOS. The isolated individual route and the combination quick pass routes are easy to learn and execute.

The interior blocking for the 118/119 play-action pass is the aggressive quick-pass technique. The individual assignments reflect the basic 18/19 play.

Center:	Over, backside LB, aggressive technique.
On Guard:	#1 outside breast, aggressive technique.
On Tackle:	#2 outside breast, aggressive technique.
Off Guard:	#1 inside breast, pivot technique.
Off Tackle:	#2 inside breast, pivot technique.

A primary adjustment in the protection scheme is in the FB assignment. The basic 18/19 requires an arc block on the perimeter. However, the 118/119 dictates an automatic load block on the end defender to clear the QB's passing lane (Diagram 9-4).

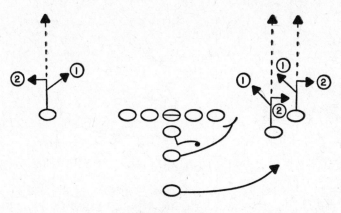

Diagram 9-4

FB:	Load block the end defender on the LOS. This is usually #3.
TB:	Sprint the pitch route to draw defensive rotation.

The QB technique also varies from the base lead option. After stepping back with the playside foot to clear the LOS, the QB maintains this depth and moves parallel to the LOS rather than attacking downhill (Diagram 9-4). This opens the QB's visual path of the route and protects him from any immediate rush. The ball is brought to a set position at the strong shoulder, rather than carried at the sternum. The base 118/119 is constructed of individual timing routes. The QB is able to deliver the ball quicker by moving toward the receiver and maintaining a parallel depth behind the LOS.

The two basic routes are diagramed in 9-4. The "1" route is the quick three-step slant. The "2" route is the four-step quick out. The individual routes are constructed to attack defensive alignment or design. An example is diagramed in 9-5. This play is spread right, 118 Z–1. The SE is assigned the "1" route, so the remaining receiver automatically releases on clearing routes. Man coverage, as diagramed in 9-5, is quickly challenged with the short crossing pass pattern.

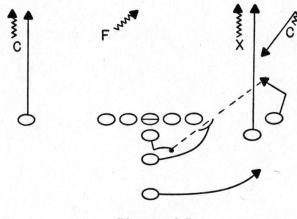

Diagram 9-5

Zone coverages that align and adjust to motion by remaining deep are vulnerable to the quick out. Diagram 9-6 illustrates Spread Right, Fly, 119 Y–2. The quick out to the SLT underneath coverage is safe and effective in creating one-on-one situations on the perimeter.

As previously mentioned, the purpose for using the lead-out action was to encourage defensive rotation toward the pseudo option flow. This rotation in the secondary leaves the quick throwback seams very vulnerable. Spread Right, 118 X–1 throwback (Diagram 9-7) is one example of slipping the quick route up the back door seam. The QB opens in the direction of the play called.

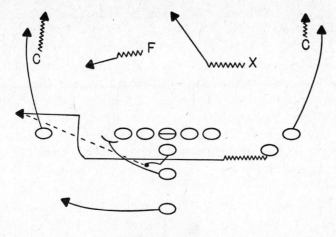

Diagram 9-6

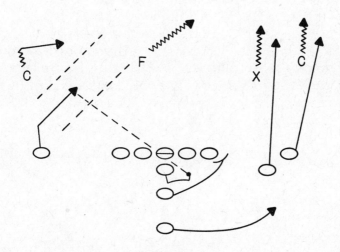

Diagram 9-7

On the second step down the LOS, the QB pivots inside, and leads the quick slant up the throwback seam in front of the corner and behind the rotating safety.

The complete possibilities for isolating receivers one-on-one in the secondary are almost unlimited. Using the clearing routes to back off coverage and then breaking a quick route underneath gives the defense a dimension other than the deep play-action pass and the option series to prepare for.

COACHING THE BOOTLEGS

The bootleg action is incorporated into the multiple option system for two reasons. First, the QB controls the football throughout the majority of the play and pressures the defense with a run/pass option at the perimeter. Both the QB's running and passing skills can be utilized. Second, the bootleg capitalizes by combining misdirection with the play-action pass. The play-action fake freezes defensive reaction, which increases the effectiveness of the misdirection. Bootlegs satisfy the big play concept demanded by the series specialties.

The 30 and 40 series are selected as the primary actions for building the bootleg specialties. The 30 series encourages immediate defensive rotation and flow to stop the triple option. The bootleg counters away from rotation to capitalize with the run/pass option. The 40 series is selected to create maximum misdirection by combining the TB counter with bootleg action.

Play 335 boot at 8 is the basic option action bootleg (Diagram 9-8). Flow begins into the weak side, then counters back toward the formation strength. The interior blocking assignments are the standard play-action design. The onside must neutralize the LOS with the aggressive technique to permit the QB to roll toward the perimeter. The Offside Tackle is assigned the #2 defender. The

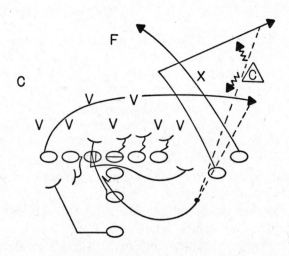

Diagram 9-8   335 Boot at 8

pivot technique keeps him up in the LOS without giving up a quick pass key. The Off Guard is assigned to arc pull to a maximum depth of six yards to gain an outside contain position on the defensive end. The pulling guard is coached to mirror the defender's charge and neutralize the rush. The FB is responsible to fill for the pulling guard. After executing the ride fake, the FB wham blocks the inside hip of the #1 defender. The TB is assigned to wham block the end man on the LOS away from the bootleg action. The TB leads his first two steps toward the sideline, crossing over on the third to attack the inside hip of the end defender.

The receiver's routes are a combination of crossing and flooding patterns. The SE is assigned to collapse the playside by driving off on a deep slant toward the near hip of the free safety. This route clears the deep middle zone while drawing the onside defenders toward the inside.

The SLT parallels the SE deep slant route. On the eighth step off the LOS, the SLT plants the inside foot and breaks under the SE clearing route toward the corner. The SLT keys the onside corner for the route's depth. If the first defender is locked up in man coverage on the SE or is hanging in the front of the zone, the SLT flattens out his break toward the sideline. This creates an easier target for the QB and a safer angle for the reception. Should the corner drop deep into the 1/3 zone, the SLT drives his inside hip, stretching the short zone for the TE drag.

The TE is assigned to release inside and drag to an eight- to twelve-yard depth behind the LBers and under the far corner. The TE is the primary receiver in this bootleg. Therefore, he is instructed to work into the horizontal seam and make himself visible by turning his shoulders slightly to the QB upon breaking past the onside tackle.

The QB's technique must sell the defense on the option play. The QB rides the FB to his belt. Once the balance step is planted, the ball is disconnected from the FB. The QB is instructed to pause momentarily to allow the FB to clear. This eliminates fumbling on the disconnect, establishes the validity of the option fake, and gives the pulling guard time to set his arc block angle on the perimeter. The QB reverses off his plant step to attack the perimeter on the bootleg action.

Once the QB begins his reversing action, he is coached to immediately snap his chin over the backfield shoulder to pick up the playside defensive rush. This quick look also gives the QB his depth perception in adjusting the guard's arc block. The ball is carried firmly with both hands in a set position as the QB sprints on the bootleg. The interior line is to show pass to open up the QB's running potential. The QB's thought process is, "I will pass unless there is no contain."

The QB's launch point is outside of the On Tackle. As he approaches the perimeter he keys the corner for his route options. If the corner drops deep, the QB is instructed to wait for the TE to clear underneath. Should the corner squat or come up on contain, the SLT becomes the secondary target. The primary advantage of this combination crossing and flood route is that if pass coverage is tight in the secondary, the QB still has his run option with a lead blocker.

The 40 series bootleg creates maximum deception by mixing the TB counter trap with the play-action pass/run option. The basic interior protection scheme is designed to simulate the TB counter. Play 443 boot at 8 (Diagram 9-9) assigns the Onside Tackle to aggressively contain the #2 defender's outside rush. The inside dive fake to the FB will help draw the defender to the inside. The Onside Guard is assigned to arc block on the perimeter specifically containing the end man on the LOS. The center aggressively attacks his base 42/43 assignment. The Off Guard and Tackle are

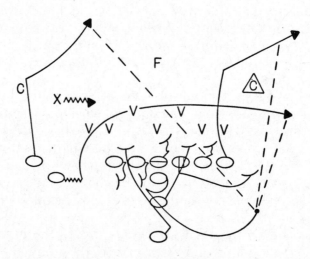

Diagram 9-9   443 Boot at 8

assigned to pivot and lock up with #1 and #2 defenders. The FB wham blocks the outside hip of the defender over the pulling guard after making a short dive fake. The TB seals the offside gap between the OG and OT after faking the trap with the QB. The protection scheme is designed to give the QB maximum time behind the LOS to execute the counter fakes on his way to the bootleg.

The basic 443 boot routes are designed to flood the playside and, in addition to the pass/run option, give the QB a deep throwback route to the SE. The TE is assigned to release inside and sprint upfield, breaking to the flag at 12 yards. Zip motion brings the SLT into a close alignment to release on a eight- to twelve-yard drag route. Both the TE and SLT key the onside corner for their route depth. The TE works into the vertical seam behind the corner's drop while the SLT looks for the horizontal seam underneath.

The SE is responsible to work into the deep throwback seam behind the free safety's rotation. This route serves two functions. First, the deep post occupies the safety's middle zone and prevents a quick rotation into the weak side to support the corner coverage. The act of preventing the safety from rotating places the corner in an option stretch situation. Second, this route gives the QB a third receiver in the bootleg action. The deep breaking post route, if unattended, becomes an immediate deep threat. The bootleg is designed to capitalize with this big play concept.

The QB's action requires an expressed degree of patience in executing an effective play-action fake before reversing toward the perimeter. The QB opens to the playside, making a quick jab fake to the FB. The completed counter action rides the TB to the LOS. The QB disconnects from the TB and reverses to the perimeter. Like the 30 series bootleg, the QB is coached to snap his head back toward the playside to locate the defensive rush.

Once at the perimeter, the QB keys the corner for the route selection. The basic bootleg concept is to select the nearest receiver as the primary target, then work upfield according to the corner's reaction. The SLT's drag is the primary route. If the corner rolls up to cover the drag, the TE becomes the secondary receiver on the breaking flag route. The third option is the deep throwback post to the SE. When the safety vacates the middle zone, the three-receiver pattern combined with the QB pass/run option makes this misdirection bootleg very effective in freezing radical defensive pursuit.

INSTALLING THE OPTION REVERSE

The option reverse is a very simple, yet effective, adjustment to the base triple option series. It is used to check defensive pursuit. The Twin alignment is especially favorable to the reverse for several reasons. The SLT is aligned in an ideal location to intercept the pitch on the way to the weak side of the formation. The SE wide alignment and downfield release does not give a hint to any adjustment. Pro formations sacrifice the downfield release when the flanker is assigned to intercept the pitch. The TE close alignment collapses the perimeter for the pulling guard and the reversing slot. The option reverse develops very quickly from the Twin alignment. Play 38 Y reverse at 9 is illustrated in Diagram 9-10 versus a base 5–2 front.

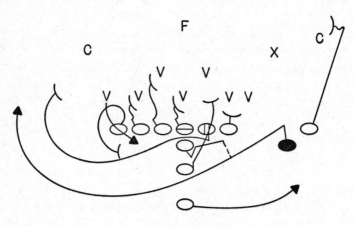

Diagram 9-10

Center:	Over, backside LB through the playside gap.
On Guard:	#1 outside breast through the playside gap.
On Tackle:	#2 outside breast through the playside gap.
TE:	Release inside, quickly peel around to the outside and gain depth. Set the pick block up two yards deep facing the oncoming SLT. Work toward the SLT, sealing off the first pursuit to commit upfield. The TE is taught to break down and let the block come to him. This prevents clipping infractions and lets the SLT set up the block.
Off Guard:	Arc pull around the playside and looking for the first defender. Get outside the TE's pick block before working

upfield. Break down and run through the outside breast of the widest defender.

Off Tackle: #2 inside breast. This block is critical in protecting the QB's pitch to the SLT. No penetration can be tolerated along the offside.

FB: Fake the dive handoff and wham block the defender over the pulling guard. Penetrate the LOS to clear the QB's downhill approach to the pitch point.

TB: Sprint the pitch route. Fake the reception and turn upfield to draw secondary pitch support.

SE: Release wide and stalk block the first defender.

SLT: Plant the first step forward to simulate a downfield release and to gain proper balance to pivot inside toward the TB's original alignment. Sprint under the TB's pitch route, keying the QB's pitch all the way. On the reception, locate the TE's pick block to assist in getting on the corner. The pulling guard is the upfield escort.

Coaching Point:

The option reverse is vulnerable to heavy stunting into the TE side of the formation. The delayed nature of all reversing plays is susceptible to penetration at the point of attack. Therefore, the SLT is coached to immediately secure the ball in the outside arm after the reception. The ball must be tightly covered until the SLT breaks outside of the TE block.

QB: Execute the basic triple ride with the FB. Disconnect and flatten out down the LOS. Throttle down after the disconnect to allow the SLT to gain an inside position on the TB. The pitch is made when the SLT is eclipsing the TB's pitch route.

The option reverse adds flair to the triple option series. The reverse play fully satisfies the eclectic concepts that belong in the multiple option package.

THE STRATEGIC USE OF FB MOTION

The terminology used to indicate FB motion is *Rip* (right) and *Liz* (left) (Diagram 9-11). Regardless of the formation's alignment,

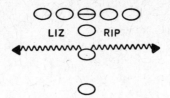

Diagram 9-11

the Rip or Liz call gives the FB his motion direction. The width of
the motion is determined by the specific play design and intent.
There are three primary reasons for including FB motion into the
series specialties. First, defenses that key the FB for the option flow
are totally disoriented when their primary key goes in motion.
Defensive keys must be shifted so that the element of confusion is
possible. Second, this motion is used to gain strategical blocking
position for the FB. Third, the Rip/Liz can be used as a decoy.

The Teen series benefits directly from the FB motion. Diagram 9-12 illustrates the FB motion versus a 5–2 inverted defense.
The Rip call places the FB outside the option point and closer to the
inverted safety, whom he is assigned to arc block and prevent from
crashing to the pitchback. This variation of the lead series is essential, especially when the FB lacks the speed to attack the perimeter
outright.

The teen load-blocking scheme is complemented by Liz motion in Diagram 9-13. Motion gives the FB an improved angle to set

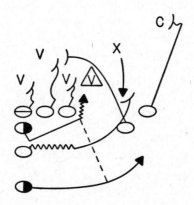

Diagram 9-12

up the load block on the crashing defensive end. The QB is now able to directly attack the perimeter on the double option.

Rip/Liz motion gives the I formation the same outside veer attack angle as does the split backfield (Diagram 9-14). A short-timed motion by the FB turns play 36/37 into the hard outside veer. The QB is granted the freedom to quickly attack the perimeter with a variation of the basic triple option. Timing is the key factor in polishing the outside veer using Rip/Liz motion. The FB is coached to take a short, two-step motion. The snap is timed for the FB's third, or plant step. On the third step, the FB pivots and landmarks the outside hip of the OT, where he meshes with the QB en route to the LOS. The basic assignments and techniques for 36/37 are not altered. The motion scheme creates a new dimension for a varia-tion of the 30 series.

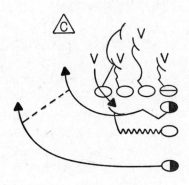

Diagram 9-13

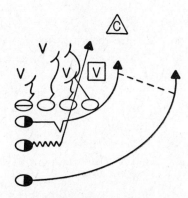

Diagram 9-14

10

OPTIONING
THE PERIMETER
WITH THE
FULL SPRINT PASS

There are three primary reasons for including the full sprint (80) series in the multiple option system. First, the open passing game softens up the defensive run support. A balanced run/pass ratio dictates the use of defensive alignments that are designed to account for each phase of the option in addition to covering each level of the passing game. The threat of a fine-tuned passing attack eliminates the overloaded run-support defensive schemes. Second, the full sprint (and the passing game in general) commits to a greater extent the receiving corps into the overall offensive design. When the perimeter receiving skills are incorporated into the total package design, this individual contribution not only balances the collective offensive objectives, but serves as a multi-dimensional motivational factor in the development of the complete disciplined unit. Third, the 80 series is an effective weapon for challenging the defensive front horizontally with the run/pass options in conjunction with the pattern combinations that stretch the secondary on the vertical scale.

Each series in the Twin-I multiple option contributes specific advantages that, when coordinated, pose strategical problems for defensive preparation. There are five advantages that the 80 series offers to the collective offensive scheme.

1. The full sprint immediately attacks the perimeter, forcing the coverage to declare itself.

2. The direction of the sprint dictates to the defense where its primary contain pressure will come from. Therefore, the types of coverages are limited to those that can condense laterally to support the sprint-out pass patterns.

3. The I formation lends itself to maximum pass blocking off tackle to aid the QB in breaking contain. This heavy blocking at the perimeter also disguises the delay routes out of the backfield in the direction of the sprint.

4. The sprint action places the QB outside of the primary pass rush. Interior protection schemes and techniques are simplified significantly since the QB is gaining passing time by moving away from the rush.

5. The 80 series places a trained running QB on the perimeter with a pass/run option. Tremendous vertical stretch can be placed on the defensive coverage when a running QB is attacking the LOS while threatening to pass.

There are disadvantages to the sprint-out attack that can be argued. The most common argument by dropback enthusiasts is that the sprint-out limits the downfield area that can be attacked. As the sprint develops, the passing field area condenses toward the sideline. There are pro and con issues for both the dropback and sprint-out series. Both are effective when tailored to complement the overall offensive philosophy. The 80 series is adopted into the multiple option philosophy, not because it is superior to any other style of passing; it is included for its compatibility to the Twin-I objectives. In terms of teaching time, preparation, and adherence to the option concepts, the full-sprint series is adequately functional.

There are four primary objectives in designing the open passing game attack for the Twin-I system. Each objective is considered for its technical merit and effect on defensive alignment and/or personnel. The type of pass coverage deployed in the secondary is as critical in structuring the passing game as option defensing assignments and schemes are to the running game design. Therefore, the complete open passing game is structured around the following four objectives.

1. Create one-on-one coverage situations in the secondary by using crossing and or timing routes.

2. Flood each perimeter zone separately to create a two-on-one or better advantage for the offense. Layer the sideline with three or more receivers to apply maximum flood pressure in the direction of the sprint.

3. Use alignments and routes that stretch the zones sufficiently to create passing seams that can be attacked both vertically and horizontally.

4. Employ clearing routes to vacate zones. Attack these vacancies with delayed-type routes.

COACHING THE 80 SERIES PROTECTION TECHNIQUES

Four primary techniques are used in structuring the full-sprint protection scheme. The onside interior technique is the standard aggressive block utilized in the play-action series. The blockers are assigned a man responsibility. The aggressive block attacks the outside breast of the defender and maintains contact up in the LOS. The objective of the aggressive technique is to prevent immediate penetration or lateral pursuit down the LOS. The QB must be given the opportunity to break contain without giving up too much depth in the backfield. The three elements of an effective aggressive block are:

1. Contact the defender's outside breast on the LOS. This is a controlled collision used to stop the initial charge. Step to the block, don't lunge.

2. Once the defender's feet are stopped, the blocker regains a playside position on the LOS. This move leaves only a rushing path *away* from the QB's sprint direction. The blocker is coached to divorce the defender after the collision. Resetting to ensure a playside position is a key factor in collapsing the onside rush.

3. Continue to pop and reset until the rush is channeled away from the playside sprint (Diagram 10-1).

The *step and hinge*, or the offside technique, is an advanced and modified pivot block. The primary objectives of the step-and-hinge block are first, protect the playside gap from stunts and immediate penetration. Next, set up the block deep enough in the backfield to delay the contact. Delaying the offside block reduces the possibilities of a quick rush chasing the QB down from behind. This delay tactic also aids the interior line in identifying and adjusting to

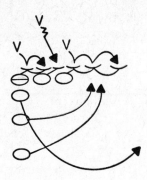

Diagram 10-1

stunts. The last objective in the step-and-hinge protection scheme is to force the rush around the backside of the block. The defensive pursuit is channeled the "long way around" before a direct course toward the QB's launch point is earned.

A composite description of the step-and-hinge technique is derived from the swinging gate concept. Diagram 10-2 illustrates the original alignment of the offside lineman. The ready position after the snap simulates a gate swinging on its hinges. The blockers maintain relative position with each other, but swing the gate back, leaving only an outside rush avenue.

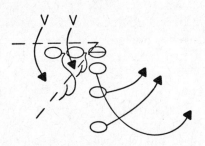

Diagram 10-2

There are four elements in executing a successful step-and-hinge technique.

1. The initial step is down the LOS to close the inside gap. This is also crucial in establishing the playside position on the rush.
2. Immediately on the initial step, the blockers pivot back and retreat into the ready position. The OT is required to hustle back

to keep the hinge relationship with the OG. In both instances, the OG and OT have reduced their inside gaps to a controllable distance.

3. The blockers break down into a ready or hitting position with their feet buzzing and their heads up. Upon retreating, the blocker is coached to be patient and let the defender come to him. The collision is made up through the defender to stop his initial momentum. The blocker divorces and regains an inside position on the defender.

4. The final element in the step and hinge is to "lock on" and drive the defender to the outside. After the blocker pops him and stops the initial rush, the defender's own rush momentum can be used to channel his pursuit to the outside. The blocker locks on the inside breast and herds the defender wide.

There are two primary blocks taught to break down the perimeter contain. The first is the FB's cut block and the second is the TB's clean-up block. The FB and the TB are assigned specific roles in the blocking scheme to prevent confusion or entanglement during the play. The FB's assignment is the primary block to seal off perimeter contain.

The FB cut block has three elements that incorporate the legality of the technique and keep the block effective. The first component is the approach to the assigned defender. The FB is coached to run a short arc path (Diagram 10-3) that intercepts the defender's outside hip. The approach is aggressively attacked to prevent the defender from gaining depth into the backfield to contain the QB sprint. The cut block is intended to be executed on or as close to the LOS as possible.

The second component in the cutblock is actual collision with the defender. The FB landmarks the defender's outside hip. The collision is made by throwing the inside elbow through the defender's outside hip. The block is initiated high to prevent the defender from straight arming and driving the block to the ground. Once contact is made, the FB slips into a four-point cross-body block.

The follow-through, or third component, requires the FB to work his head upfield to cut off the defender's lateral pursuit. The cut block cannot reduce itself completely to the ground. Once the block is into the defender's legs, constant pressure is applied by staying alive on all four points (the "crab" block).

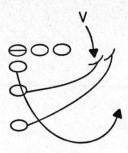

Diagram 10-3

The TB's clean-up block is designed to be a secondary support for the FB cut block. The TB parallels the FB short arc path to gain outside leverage on the assigned defender (Diagram 10-3). Once the FB throws the cut block, the TB works into position to attack the defender's outside breast. The TB is coached to reset after the collision and to keep a position between the rush and the QB. The clean-up assignment serves three practical purposes for the 80 series protection scheme. First, should the contain defender break through the cut block, the TB is a secondary line of protection. Second, should the cut block contain the rush, the TB can turn back to the inside to pick up a rush from the backside or key on expected stunts. Third, the TB's arc path and commitment into the LOS combine to create delay route possibilities.

Diagrams 10-4 and 10-5 illustrate the combined base 80 series protection assignments.

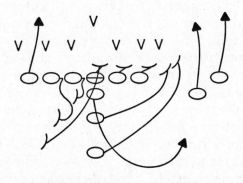

Diagram 10-4   Vs. 6–1

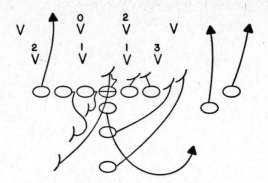

Diagram 10-5   Vs. 44 Stack

Center:	Over, backside LB. Backdoor assignment if uncovered.
On Guard:	#1 outside breast, aggressive technique.
On Tackle:	#2 outside breast, aggressive technique.
Off Guard:	#1 step and hinge.
Off Tackle:	#2 step and hinge.
TB:	Clean-up block at the perimeter if "Max" protection is designated.

OPTIONING THE STRONGSIDE CORNER

Two basic pass plays are utilized to attack into the strongside perimeter. The first is a timing pattern that creates vertical seams. The second is a strongside flood that layers the sideline at four different depths. In both cases, the strongside corner is the primary key that determines route adjustments and the selected receiver. It is important to note at this point, that although the QB is drilled to think and look pass first, the run option is a preferred alternative to forcing a bad pass or stopping on the LOS to wait for a route to clear. The 80 series is a continuous action that attacks toward and beyond the LOS.

Play 84/85 (Diagram 10-6) constitutes a timed sideline route to the SE as the primary target. The SE releases two yards wide of the first defender and drives twelve steps off the LOS. The SE plants and drives back three yards toward the sideline. The SE anticipates the pass by snapping his head around on the plant step to locate the ball in flight. This timed sideline route places tremendous coverage pressure on the corner regardless of his man or zone assignment.

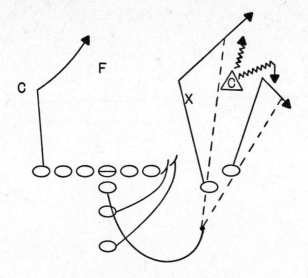

Diagram 10-6   84/85 Vs. 4 Deep

The SLT is assigned the flag route but his break and route depth are dependent upon the strong corner's reaction to the SE sideline route. The SLT releases directly at the second defender. As the SLT drives upfield, he keys the SE for the sideline plant step. Once the SE plants, the SLT breaks toward the flag. If the corner is dropping deep, the SLT drives to his inside hip to draw coverage and prevent the corner from rotating forward to the sideline route. Should the corner stick tight to the sideline routes, the SLT flattens his route into the upfield vertical seam. The flag route becomes the secondary target when the corner rotates forward to cover the SE on the sideline. The combination of a timed route underneath the corner and the breaking flag pattern behind, in conjunction with the threat of a QB keep, creates coverage decisions at the perimeter.

The primary coverage threat for 84/85 is a heavy rotation with the free safety going over the top to cover the flag. This move would release the strong corner from his deep coverage assignment and allow closer positioning to counter the timed sideline route. The TE becomes instrumental in forcing the coverage to balance up in its rotation and zone coverage responsibilities. The TE is designated to run a post route that landmarks the deep seam in between the free safety's rotating action and the weakside corner. This deep post is an immediate deep threat to an overaggressive or heavy rotating secondary. The post is designed primarily as a decoy. However, its inclusion as a preselected adjustment to the basic 84/85 is illustrated in Diagram 10-7 versus a four-deep secondary that condenses toward the strong side to defend the timing route by overrotating.

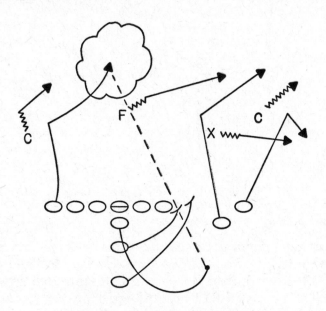

Diagram 10-7   Right 84 X Post

The QB's thought process for executing 84/85 is, "I will throw the sideline route unless the corner commits up." The timed sideline route is the first priority. However, should the corner tighten coverage, the QB's second option is to go over the top to the breaking flag route by the SLT. In either case, the sprint action is continuous toward the LOS. The QB's third option is the run.

Diagram 10-8 illustrates the basic flood pass. Play 88/89 is designed to layer the strong sideline. Four receivers are released into the pattern to overload the strongside zones. The SE is assigned a deep 30-yard comeback. This is primarily a clearing route to challenge the deep outside 1/3 zone. The SE drives deep up the sideline taking the corner as deep as possible. If corner coverage remains tight, the SE continues to drive upfield. Should the corner drop his coverage, the SE is coached to work in behind and fade toward the sideline.

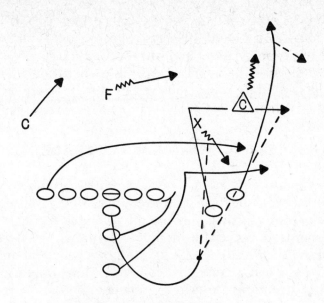

Diagram 10-8   Right 88 Vs. 4 Deep

The TB is assigned to release immediately into the flat zone to draw coverage. His five-yard route is designed to compound the vertical stretch on the sideline. Combining the SE deep route along the sideline with the TB short route in the flat creates a horizontal seam in the strongside perimeter.

The SLT is the primary receiver for 88/89. He is assigned to drive toward the defender's inside hip to a depth of twelve steps. Depending upon the length of the stride, twelve steps generally places the sideline break between 16 and 22 yards. At twelve steps, the SLT breaks toward the sideline, working for the open spots in the perimeter coverage.

The TE is assigned to release inside and drag across the field. His route depth is determined by the strongside flat coverage. The TE reads the defender that is covering the TB in the flat and then works in behind. As a general rule, the TE drag can expect to drift into the eight- to ten-yard range. The drag timing with relation to the sideline route is delayed slightly, which permits the SLT to enter the back of the horizontal seam first. He is followed by the TE dragging into the bottom of the seam. The intent of this flood pattern is to give the QB as many receivers as possible in a continuous throwing line. All the receivers are lined up along the sideline, which eliminates any visual searching for the QB.

The QB's primary target on the full sprint is the SLT on the sideline break. His thought process is geared to key the corner's coverage response. As the QB sprints out, his thought process is, "I will throw the sideline break unless the corner hangs." The TE drag is the secondary route, followed by the SE's deep comeback behind the corner.

BEATING WEAKSIDE COVERAGE

The basic design of the twin alignment complements the sprint-out pass into the formation strength. Defenses must prepare to cover the route possibilities from the twin receiver alignment in their design and especially in their alignment. The weakside sprint-out is designed to balance up the attack with relation to field perspective and to capitalize on defensive alignments that are over-cautious in defending the twin alignment.

Diagram 10-9 illustrates the basic weakside flood. Play 80/81 layers the weakside of the formation with three receivers. The TE releases outside with the intention of breaking the flag route at 15 yards. He keys the corner for the final depth break. The flag route is intended to drive the corner deep in an attempt to open a horizontal seam for the SLT on the drag route. However, should the corner roll up and leave coverage, the TE is instructed to bend

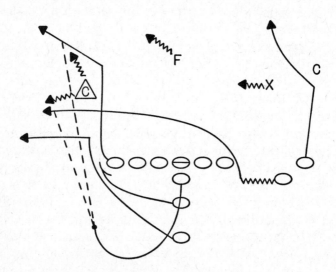

Diagram 10-9   Right Zip 81

toward the sideline before the rotating safety can gain a coverage position.

As in the strongside flood play, the TB is assigned to release immediately into a shallow flat route to draw coverage. This route completes the vertical stretch on the weakside perimeter. Once the TB reaches the sideline, he is instructed to hook up and face the QB, creating a short zone dump target or a legal receiver to overthrow.

Zip motion is used to bring the SLT into a quick release alignment. The SLT keys the corner's reaction to the stretch and works into the vacancy. Should the corner lock up man-to-man with the TE or drop into a deep zone, the SLT works underneath looking for the quick pass. If roll coverage develops, the SLT occupies the corner to open up the TE, bending back under the free safety's rotation.

The SE strongside post is a decoy route to keep the secondary from overcompensating toward the sprint flow. The SE is coached to break the nine-step post directly at the free safety in an attempt to force the deep middle 1/3 coverage to stay home.

This weakside flood gives the QB a basic corner read. The primary receiver for 80/81 is the drag by the SLT. Should the corner hang to cover the drag, the TE flag becomes the secondary target. The flood routes develop quickly into the weak side of the formation; therefore, the pass/run threat is especially effective in forcing the secondary to declare its coverage.

Weakside coverage more often than not results in a corner rotation and a mass condensing of the deep zones in the direction of the sprint. Thus, a combination of clearing and throwback routes is effective in checking the secondary's exodus toward the weakside flood. Diagram 10-10 illustrates the primary adjustment to the base 80/81 weakside sprint.

Zip motion is also used to keep in harmony with the base design. The weakside sprint and the stretching routes are executed to draw coverage. The SLT is assigned, however, to alter his route and break the post toward the free safety. The objective of the post route is to drive the free safety as deep as possible. This, in turn, opens up both the horizontal seam behind the inside LBers for the SE drag and the vertical seam for the TE flag over the corner and in front of the safety.

The QB sprint mechanics are modified to accommodate the throwback scheme. It is imperative that the QB attack the perime-

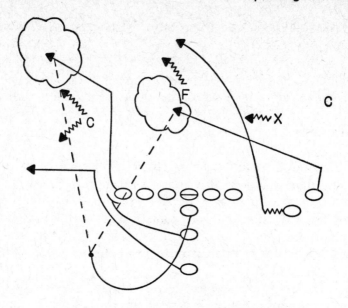

Diagram 10-10   Right Zip 81 Throwback

ter with full enthusiasm. Failure to do so slows down the anticipated rotation in the secondary and congests the throwback seams. Once the QB achieves an outside sprint approach toward the LOS, he is coached to pull up and turn back to the inside to locate and key the free safety's reaction.

The primary objective is to isolate the SE on the drag under the safety's rotation. This throwback route is generally obscured from the underneath LB coverage. The sprint action encourages the short zone defenders to condense laterally, thus focusing their attention in the sprint direction. The drag route slips in the back door relatively unnoticed. If the throwback seam is congested, the QB shifts to his secondary target, the TE on the flag route. The two deep routes by the TE and SLT in conjunction with the full-sprint action challenge the deep safety's coverage assignment. Combining the weakside flood with its throwback adjustments satisfies the need to attack both sides of the formation and a vast proportion of the field with the open passing game.

COACHING THE FULL-SPRINT SCREEN AND DRAW

Both the full-sprint throwback screen and the cutback draw serve as equalizers in the 80 series scheme. The sprint action encourages defensive movement and rotation. The screen and draw counter defensive adjustments after the snap by attacking from the opposite direction of the sprint flow.

Right 88 3 screen at 7 (Diagram 10-11) is included in the sprint series package for three reasons.

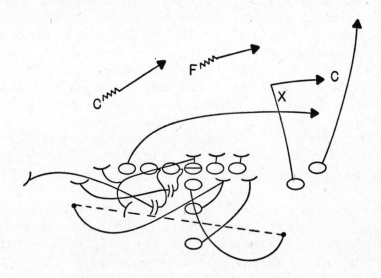

Diagram 10-11   Right 88 3 Screen at 7

1. The throwback screen capitalizes quickly on the weakside cover-age that condenses toward the direction of the sprint. The basic 88 flood routes are designed to pull coverage away from the screen development. The screen slips out the back door to challenge the weakside coverage.

2. The weakside screen slows down the trailing pass rush. Crashing defensive ends that are assigned to chase down the QB complement the screen objectives.

3. The screen play gives the offensive line an opportunity to escape the standard protection assignments and venture into a different perspective in pass blocking. This diversification breeds enthusiasm and is a healthy adjustment for the interior line.

The mechanics of the FB screen mirror the base 88/89 play, with the exception of the offside screen-blocking techniques and the backfield protection scheme. The screen blocking develops after the offside has set up in the step-and-hinge technique. After a "1,001–1,002" count, the tackle is assigned to release straight down the LOS, looking for the widest defender that appears. The tackle is responsible to kick out any pursuit that develops from the outside-in. The guard is the FB's personal escort. He releases down the LOS to a spot just wide of the TE's original alignment. The guard is responsible to shield the FB's reception and lead on the first defender to appear on the FB's command. The center has an inside pursuit assignment. As the center releases down the LOS, he is instructed to check over the backfield shoulder for pursuit following the FB's lateral release. The center sets up a pick block to allow the FB to break open just wide of the perimeter. If the FB slips out the back door unattended, the center is assigned to turn upfield aside the guard and seal the first pursuit that develops from the inside.

There are three key coaching points in teaching the throw-back screen-blocking scheme. First, the blockers must step and hinge the full two counts to draw the rush. The sprint-out must appear authentic. Second, the interior unit must release simultaneously down the LOS. This release must be smooth and consistent. The FB's timing depends upon the positioning of the screen blocks. Uniformity is imperative. Thirdly, it is impossible to predict where defensive interference will come from. Therefore, the primary screen rule for the interior three blockers is, "Never pass up the opposite color after the release down the LOS."

The TB is assigned to cut block at the perimeter to assist the QB in breaking contain in addition to protecting the launch point. The FB is instructed to step up into the OG-OT gap simulating 80 series strongside protection and delay the full two counts. On the second count, the FB slips down the LOS in behind the rush. The FB is coached to gain enough depth off the LOS to permit an inside turn back toward the QB. The inside turn is designed to give the FB a clear view of the LOS before receiving the football. The FB acknowledges the reception to begin the blocking surge upfield.

The QB's sprint technique must sell the defense on the downfield pass threat. After opening at six o'clock, the QB shoulders the ball and sprints out, focusing completely away from the developing screen. Once the QB breaks the tackle position, he should be at the maximum sprint depth. The QB pulls up and pauses to draw maximum rush. Only after hesitating a single count does the QB pivot inside to locate the FB and complete the screen pass.

The 84/85 draw is included in the full-sprint package primarily to slow down the interior rush and to utilize the running skills of the TB. The objective of the draw is to bait defensive rotation in the direction of the sprint and then counter with a delayed handoff to the TB, who is assigned to break back against the flow reading daylight (Diagram 10-12).

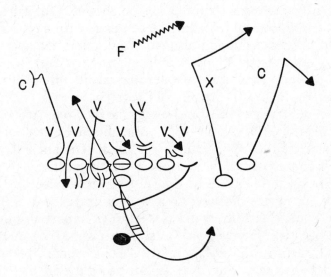

Diagram 10-12 Right 84 Draw Vs. Odd Front

The basic 84/85 routes (with the exception of the TE) are used to encourage a full rotation away from the draw. The TE releases directly for the weakside corner in an attempt to drive him deep. As long as the corner respects the TE release, he is not an immediate threat to the draw. The TE is instructed to stalk the corner once the draw is recognized.

The interior blocking design is intended to open the cutback alley over the first LBer bubble from the inside-out toward the weak side. There are two basic rules for technique selection. The first is the "covered" rule, the second is the "uncovered" rule.

The "covered" rule gives reference to the linemen who are covered by a down position defender either head-up or in the immediate outside gap. The covered rule indicates that the blocker use a quick pivot technique. This technique (described earlier for play-action passing) gives the down defenders an immediate rush path to the outside. Once the rush begins, the blockers lock on and drive the defender away from the cutback alley. The defenders are popped immediately after taking the inside pivot step. This keeps the rush channeled to the outside and widens the cutback seam toward the LB bubble. The covered center is the exception to the rule. In the event the center is covered or shaded to either side, he is instructed to give the nose guard a free rush path in any desired direction. The center is then required to step into the rush and gain an inside position between the defender and the ball. The center, like other covered linemen, is instructed to lock on and ride the defender away from the draw crease.

The "uncovered" rule dictates that any lineman who is faced or shaded with a LBer or any defender positioned off the LOS should close the inside gap and set up showing pass protection for two full counts. On the second count, the blocker is coached to explode across the LOS and lock on the LBer and drive upfield to maintain contact. Acting is a vital element in executing a draw block technique. If the uncovered lineman can influence the LBer to begin his drop, the draw block is halfway completed.

Diagram 10-12 illustrates the 84 draw versus an odd front. The cutback alley is designed to break back over the weak inside LB. The center, however, has the critical block that gives the TB his final daylight read. The draw against an even front (Diagram 10-13) is designed to challenge the LB blocked by the center. The guards now carry the primary responsibility of decoying the inside rush around the draw alley.

The FB is assigned to block the inside breast of the #3 defender. This kick block prevents any immediate interference by protecting the exchange and the TB's initial movement into the LOS.

The TB receives the exchange by lead stepping directly at the #3 defender. This step clears the QB's six o'clock sprint opening. After the lead step, the TB squares up to the LOS and casually breaks down as if anticipating a block. The TB makes no attempt to move toward or reach for the ball. Only after the ball is replaced in the TB's hands does the cutback action begin. The TB is now instructed to break back against the flow, covering the ball with both hands and reading daylight.

The QB's mechanics require that the pass key be given quickly. The ball is quickly shouldered on the opening step as the

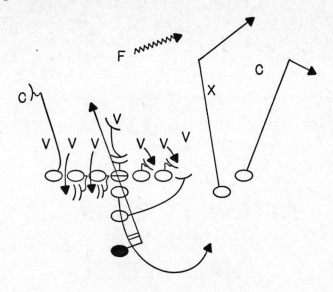

Diagram 10-13   Vs. Even Front

QB begins the sprint action. The QB is coached to brush the inside hip of the TB while simultaneously placing the ball in the TB's pouch. After the exchange, the QB carries out the full sprint fake.

The completed draw play is a combination of "sucker blocking" up front with a delayed exchange in the backfield from off of the full sprint action. Both the draw and the throwback screen complement the 80 series objectives by slowing down pursuit and rotation in the direction of the sprint. Neither the screen nor the draw is the focal point of the 80 series, but each contributes to the development of the full-sprint objectives.

11

ATTACKING DEFENSES
WITH THE
HALF SPRINT

I t is important to state that the half sprint or 70 series is an adjustment to complement the full sprint attack. The half sprint is designed to balance the complete passing game. But yet, as a supplement, the 70 series occupies a critical portion in the total passing package. The objectives of the half sprint series are designed to capitalize on a defensive structure that has been conditioned to respond to full sprint coverage. Primarily, the logic for preparing to defend a sprint-out attack versus a dropback is drastically different. Having a sprint-out QB suddenly pull up in a pocket to pass is disorienting to defenses that have been drilled to condense zones or tighten coverages to compensate for the full sprint threat.

TEACHING THE MECHANICS OF THE 70 SERIES

The mechanics of the 70 series set the QB's launch point behind the strongside tackle (Diagram 11-1). The QB sets into the strong side of the formation for three primary reasons. First, the half sprint simulates the full sprint for the first five steps. The drop step and lateral movement toward the launch point initially give the secondary the full sprint key. Second, setting up behind the strong-

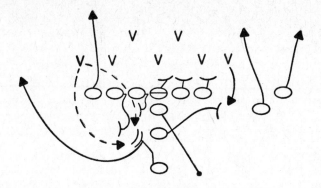

Diagram 11-1

side tackle adjusts the QB's launch point closer to the center of the formation alignment. Having the QB move toward the twin receiver alignment balances the throwing distances to the quick receivers in addition to opening up a broader attack perspective over the complete field. The third reason for including the half sprint set is to give a drilled running QB an escape route to the outside where he can effectively attack the perimeter. The half sprint set moves the QB away from the weakside rush and gives him an outside sprint option as an escape route.

The primary objective of the 70 series is to challenge the short and intermediate zones with a controlled passing attack. Clearing routes are used to open up the medium range timing patterns. A tremendous amount of practice time is required to perfect a pure dropback passing series. The 70 series borrows from the dropback scheme but tailors the design to fit a simple format that can be polished with minimal practice time.

Practice time is conserved in the development of the half-sprint protection techniques. The 70 series interior protection assignments are identical to the 80 series. The center, Onside Guard, and Onside Tackle are drilled in executing the aggressive block that keeps the rush contained near the LOS. The offside guard and tackle are assigned to delay their contact with a step-and-hinge technique. The only adjustments in the 70 series protection that vary from the 80 series are the backfield assignments.

The FB is assigned to seal the #3 defender to the playside. The approach is a direct inside-out path that gives the FB an inside position on the pass rush. The objective of the FB's seal block is to pop the defender as near to the LOS as possible. The block is executed by lowering and widening the FB's base before contact. Once the FB is in position to pop the defender, he breaks down into a hitting position and explodes up through the rush. Immediately after contact, the FB divorces the block, resets, and regains an inside position. The FB is instructed not to attempt to dominate the defender, but to slow his momentum and then channel the rush wide of the QB's launch point. An overaggressive seal block is easily side-stepped.

The TB is assigned the first LB from the outside-in to the weak side of the formation. On the snap of the ball, the TB takes three quick steps up toward the offside guard while reading the outside LB. If the assigned LB stunts inside or rushes outside (Diagram 11-1), the TB has an inside position to intercept and channel the defender to the outside, away from the QB set. Should the assigned LB drop into coverage, the TB releases out the backdoor 6–8 yards wide of the TE on the "up" route. This up route, as will be explained shortly, serves two primary functions. First, the TB release draws weakside coverage to support the strongside base 70/71 play. Second, the up route is the primary target for the weakside counterpart 72/73. Diagram 11-2 illustrates the completed 70 protection scheme versus a stunting 5–2 defense. The TB releases out the backdoor since no outside rush develops.

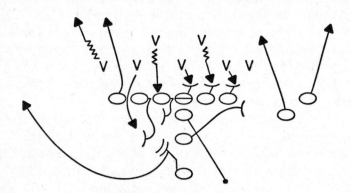

Diagram 11-2   Vs. 5–2

INCORPORATING THE THROWING LANE CONCEPT

The throwing lane concept is a method of opening up a short or intermediate zone. The primary object in constructing the throwing lane is to use a single clear route to stretch either the strong or the weak side of the formation in the anticipation of creating a horizontal seam. A short zone defender is isolated in the horizontal seam, where the perimeter boundaries of his zone can be attacked with a primary and secondary receiver.

It is vital to point out that the throwing lane concept is based on the assumption that each coverage faced will be a type of zone. Therefore, a pattern design is critical to open the horizontal seams into either the strong or weak side of the formation. Should man or a combination coverage surface, the basic patterns are effective without major adjustments. Three factors are considered in the overall development of the primary receiver. Like the base option thought process, the QB is drilled to anticipate passing to the primary receiver. Next, a secondary receiver is assigned to complete the option thought process. Lastly, a safety valve route is determined. This gives the QB an additional opportunity for a completion or a legal overthrow of the football to avoid complications.

The throwing lane concept can be examined in the base strongside half-sprint play 70/71 (Diagram 11-3). The SE is assigned a nine-step curl route. The curl route is also the primary target. The SE releases wide of the first defender and drives upfield nine steps. On the final step, the SE pivots to the inside, expecting to focus on the ball in flight. The curl route brings the

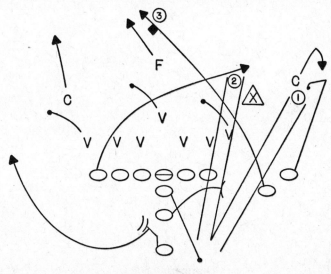

Diagram 11-3

receiver back to the ball and under perimeter coverage. If the ball
has not been thrown, the SE is coached to break down and slide
inside to give the QB a broad target.

The SLT is responsible to drive the free safety deep. This
deep slant route is designed to open up an intermediate horizontal
seam for the TE to work into. The SLT's deep route also serves as
the safety valve. The TE is assigned to release inside and drag in
immediately behind the LB drops, looking for the seam created by
the SLT release between the strong and the free safety. The drag
route serves as the secondary target.

The objective in combining the curl and drag routes is to place
the strong safety in a read situation. The QB is instructed to read
the strong safety's reaction and to pass to the receiver whose throwing lane is clear. Diagram 11-4 illustrates the safety dropping with
the SLT's clear route. Regardless of the type of coverage, the
safety's reaction has cleared the throwing lane to the SE curl. The
QB is able to determine the safety's intention on the third step. By
the fifth setting step, the QB already knows that the curl will be
thrown. Therefore, the pass can be in flight by the time the SE
plants his ninth step and pivots inside. The timed curl is difficult to
defend from behind. Therefore, the QB is instructed to focus on
the SE's inside hip as the strike point. When the SE pivots inside
toward the LOS, the pass keeps the receiver's profile low and
protected.

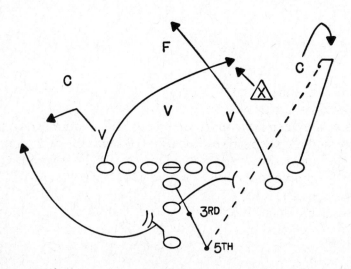

Diagram 11-4

Diagram 11-5 illustrates the strong safety flattening out into short zone coverage. His reaction cuts off the curl, but now vacates the throwing lane to the dragging TE. A key coaching point is to instruct the TE to read the safety's reaction. The TE is now able to adjust his route to work into the vacated seam left by the inverting safety. The TE is instructed to make himself visible to the QB by raising his hand as he breaks into the throwing lane. The drag, as the secondary route, gives the QB time to set up square to the LOS after reading the safety's reaction, and to anticipate the TE breaking into the throwing lane.

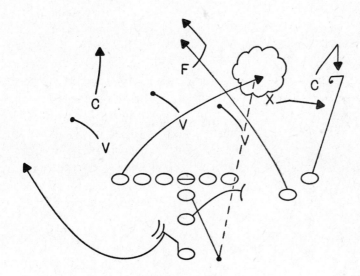

Diagram 11-5

A radical shift in coverage toward the formation strength congests both the curl and drag throwing lanes (Diagram 11-6). Therefore, the deep clearing route by the SLT generally develops into an immediate deep strike. Once the QB reads the overrotation, his final option is to locate the deep slant behind the free safety and attempt the completion, overthrow the safety valve to prevent loss of yardage, or break contain and scramble.

Play 72/73 (Diagram 11-7) is included to complement the base 70/71. One objective in setting the QB into the strength of the formation is to encourage defensive rotation in the same direction. Play 72/73 is designed to attack into the weak side of the formation away from the secondary's rotation. Initially, the routes and

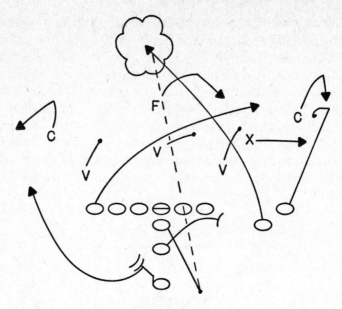

Diagram 11-6

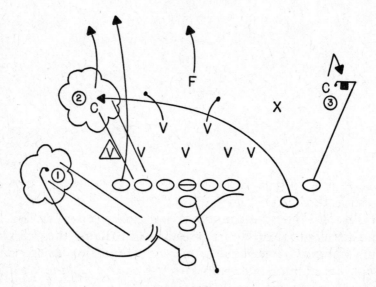

Diagram 11-7

mechanics of the weakside play simulate the base 70/71. However, the final adjustments create a weakside stretch on the perimeter.

The TE is assigned to release inside and bend directly toward the near corner's hip. The TE is responsible for creating the horizontal seam by driving the corner deep. The primary receiver is the TB releasing on a delayed up route from out of the backfield. The TB is instructed to step up toward the outside hip of the OT for two full counts. If the first LBer from the outside-in is rushing, the TB widens his route and expects the quick dump pass from the QB. The objective in stepping up and delaying the release is to force any inside LBer that may have back-out assignment to drop. This move gives the TB an outside position on the perimeter to make a quick reception without immediate coverage. If the TB reads no rush from the outside LB, he releases eight yards wide of the TE align-ment. When the TB crosses the LOS, he is instructed to turn inside at a depth of four yards and face the QB (Diagram 11-8). This route completes the shallow stretch on the weakside perimeter.

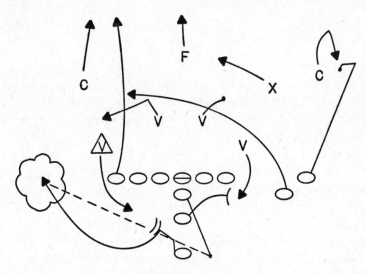

Diagram 11-8

The SLT is designated as the secondary receiver for 72/73. His release drives toward the free safety as if running the clear route for 70/71. Once the SLT breaks in behind the inside LB drops, he is instructed to flatten his route toward the weak sideline. This deep across route is intended to work in behind the outside LBer's drop, wide of the inside LBer's drop, and under the corner's deep re-treat. The soft spot in the weakside seam generally develops any-where from 12 to 18 yards deep (Diagram 11-9).

The SE executes the basic 70/71 curl with one exception. The curl is now the safety valve route; therefore, the SE must make an attempt to move back into the QB's field of vision. The SE is

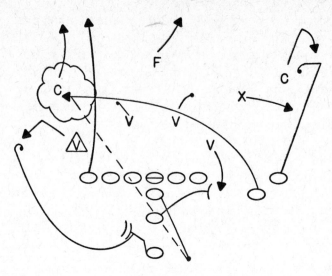

Diagram 11-9

instructed to float back to the inside looking for an open throwing lane. In addition to floating while the QB is set, the SE must be ready to break toward the sideline in the event the QB is forced to scramble outside of contain.

The play right 72 as diagramed in 11-7 requires the QB to take a seven-step drop toward the strength of the formation. The extra two steps give the receivers time to break into the developing weakside stretch. On the seventh step, the QB quickly pivots back toward the throwing lanes to read the first LB from the outside-in. Since this LB is unblocked, the QB is instructed to always expect a weakside rush. Therefore, the dump pass to the TB on the up route is the primary target (Diagram 11-8).

Once the weakside LB is located, his reaction to pass coverage ultimately determines the QB's throwing lane choices. Diagram 11-9 illustrates the LB dropping into flat coverage and intercepting the TB. The SLT is now regarded as the secondary target. The QB adjusts his visual scan into the intermediate weakside seam that the TE creates with his clearing route.

As mentioned earlier, a primary advantage of setting the QB into the formation strength is to encourage secondary coverage to conform in a like manner. In the event that a weakside roll in the secondary does develop, the SE is now isolated one-on-one into the strength of the formation (Diagram 11-10). The SE now has ample room to adjust his curl route to work into the QB's line of vision.

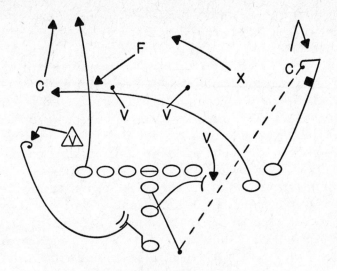

Diagram 11-10

Together, the strong- and weakside half-sprint series add yet another dimension to the multiple option concept. These two correlated patterns give the offense a simple, yet effective, broad-based pass attack. The full-sprint series encourages radical adjustments in the secondary to account for the QB's pass/run threat. The 70 series capitalizes on this conditioned reaction by attacking quickly into the strength of the coverage in addition to threatening any vacancies in the weakside adjustments.

INSTALLING THE QB DRAW

The base 70 series action is conducive to setting up a delayed cutback draw for the QB. The weak side of the formation is the ideal target for the cutback action because the defensive front is less likely to reduce itself into the TE side. The base 70 action is designed to draw the primary pursuit down the LOS. Cutback lanes for draw blocking schemes develop immediately along the weak side of the formation.

The QB draw is included into the 70 series for two primary reasons. First, the draw takes immediate advantage of the hard outside pass rush designed to contain the full sprint. Second, the draw keeps the ball in the possession of a ball carrier who is trained to be a running threat.

The interior blocking scheme for 70/71 QB draw is identical to the full-sprint draw illustrated in Chapter 10. The intent is to reduce and condense assignment learning. The interior linemen are responsible for the draw blocking techniques described in the covered and uncovered rules for the full-sprint draw. The objective in the scheme is to channel the weakside rush around the intended cutback lane. The TE is assigned to release upfield and stalk block the weakside corner. The SLT drives the free safety deep and stalks to complete the downfield blocking scheme. Both the FB and TB split toward their 70 series assignments to prevent crashing ends from prematurely forcing the QB back into the LOS.

The QB mechanics are a combination of acting and reading. The QB is instructed to open toward the strong side, setting the ball high on the shoulder to show pass. It is vital that the QB give a good pass look by focusing toward the SE. This visual contact convinces the defensive interior personnel to begin their pass drops. On the third step from scrimmage, the QB plants and momentarily sets the ball. It is at this point that the QB pivots back to the inside, tucks the ball under his arm, and breaks back under the weakside pass rush.

It is imperative that the QB sell the defense on the pass read before cutting back on the draw. Effective draw blocking techniques are dependent upon the defense committing to a pass-reaction key. The QB is instructed to be patient when setting at a three-step depth to allow the draw blocking to develop and open the cutback lanes. Diagram 11-11 illustrates the cutback lane over a weakside 5–2 LB. Diagram 11-12 points out a cutback lane over the center directly at a 4–3 inside LB. In either situation, the QB draw is an easy and yet effective method of baiting defensive reaction and then countering with a delay inside QB keep.

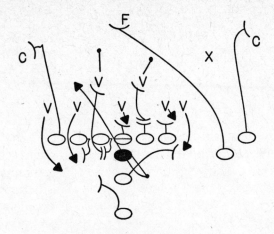

Diagram 11-11

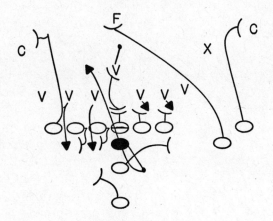

Diagram 11-12

INDEX